# BEHIND THE CURTAIN

## A Practical Introduction to How Theatre Works

## First Edition

**Tim Joyce**

Buffalo State College

**cognella**®
academic publishing

x

Bassim Hamadeh, CEO and Publisher
Michael Simpson, Vice President of Acquisitions
Jamie Giganti, Managing Editor
Jess Busch, Graphic Design Supervisor
John Remington, Acquisitions Editor
Brian Fahey, Licensing Associate
Kate McKellar, Interior Designer

Connie Joyce, Photo Editor

First published in the United States of America in 2014 by Cognella, Inc.

Cover image: Copyright © 2010 by Depositphotos / Irina Pussep.
        Copyright © 2010 by Depositphotos / Qing Gao.

Printed in the United States of America

ISBN: 978-1-62661-784-1 (pbk) / 978-1-62661-785-8 (br)

www.cognella.com        800-200-3908

# contents

## part two: theatre—the space, style, and history

part one: the **page** to the **stage**

a s the house lights finally begin to dim and the last of the reluctant cell phones are switched off, the anticipation both in front of and behind the curtain reaches a peak. The Play is starting. The culmination of a massive collaboration between artists, technicians, marketers, and volunteers; from the playwright down to the staff who cleans the theatre overnight, it has all come down to tonight. This particular performance, this presentation of the story, will only happen once. When the play ends in an hour or two and everyone goes home, that will be it. There will never be a repeat of the show that happened on this particular day. You've entered a museum where every day the paintings are repainted, recreated by the artists. That is theatre. Yes, there will be other performances in the run, there may be thousands,[1] but this one night, this one event, will disappear into the ether. And then …

Tomorrow night everyone will meet at the theatre to do it again.

This ephemeral quality is unique to the theatre. It only happens once. It happens night after night after night. Sometimes it even happens twice in one day if there

# introduction

is a matinee. It will be the same show but never the same work of art. Buy a ticket to tomorrow's performance and you will see the same actors saying the same lines. You will see the same lighting, staging, props, and costumes. You may even sit in the same seat from the evening before. It will all seem totally familiar, but simultaneously it will be completely new and different. Making it happen night after night is the task of the Theatre Company. For the actors, shrugging off both the good and bad performances is essential to the craft because, like a baseball player, you are only as good as your last at-bat. Each show you do is just one inning in a game that may never end. Making this all work takes commitment and training. It takes talent. It takes willingness to risk failure. Most of all, it takes collaboration among many artists and technicians. Everyone has to be in the same world—the world of the play—for this collaboration to sparkle. Collaboration seems like something that would be simple, obvious, and achievable time after time. But there are traps inherent to it. The artists and technicians and business people work and study and fall and fail and get up again throughout their careers, and the falling and failing more often

---

1   Thousands is by no means an exaggeration either. More than ninety Broadway shows have had more than 1,000 performances, including *Phantom of the Opera*, which as of this writing was approaching its *10,000*[th] performance on Broadway. This doesn't even include the regional touring productions of these shows.

than not can be traced to a breakdown in collaboration and the communication it takes for it to occur. Sharing and trusting the ideas of others is, in fact, not an instinct for most people, and frankly it is something that often goes against the inner egotistical urge that leads a person to desire a career in theatre in the first place. Sharing credit takes maturity and dedication to the larger art. Sharing credit is easy when the play is fantastic. Sharing the blame when the play just plain doesn't work, well … So ultimately, there's no way around this fact: Great theatre results from great collaboration among many people with specialized skills and talents. Every person who has contributed to this book will tell you this about theatre: When it all clicks, it is incredible and moving and perhaps even life changing. When there is a great performance of a well-written, directed, acted, designed, and constructed play, that night in the theatre is truly a spiritual event.

And then tomorrow night …

## what is theatre?

It is not linguistic gymnastics to say that this question has no answer, because it has infinite answers. If the student reading this book were to read every text they could find on the subject and then ask every theatrical professional or dedicated amateur to answer the question 'WHAT IS THEATRE?' that student would get virtually unlimited replies, many of which would completely contradict each other. Paradoxically, those antithetical points of view would, for the most part, *all be correct*. Theatre is a live performance, and it can take place in a billion-dollar venue or a dimly lit alley. It may have an incredibly complex script, or it may be improvised or even use no words whatsoever. There may be elaborate costuming and lighting, or it may be done with the actors naked and illuminated by nothing more than moonlight. All of these live performances legitimately qualify as residents living under the common roof of "theatre." If this sounds evasive, the authors apologize, because we are not evading the question at all. The reader must understand that *theatre is art, and art does not have a single definition that can be easily fit into a standardized "fill-in-the-blank" exam.* Anyone who has ever walked through the Modern Wing of an art museum and looked at a Jackson Pollock knows that not every work by an artist speaks to everyone. If the Pollock piece you see doesn't move you, then you might be tempted to declare, as many people do when they see abstract work, "This isn't art." The person standing next to you who has been emotionally moved by the canvas you just dismissed might angrily disagree. You are both wrong, you are both right. The same goes for theatre. Whilst sitting in the audience of an avant-garde wordless theatre piece, you might be left totally unmoved or weeping with joy. Your emotional and intellectual response, as an audience member, matters. *Your reaction* determines individually what you perceive as art, or at least effective art. You are the Arbiter; all that the members of the theatre company can hope is that they reach you emotionally or intellectually in some way.

In all the books and among all of the conversations you might have with the people of the theatre, there are, despite the "defining art" conundrum, certain things that most people *will agree on* when asked for their definition of theatre. There is a fairly strong consensus that theatre is storytelling.[2] The majority of theatre a person will see in a lifetime has a tale to tell about characters in a specific world; a time and place that is contained in the theatre space during the performance of the play. One thing that almost no one would disagree about is that theatre is live. Each performance only happens once, although, again, there may be many, many performances.[3] The final aspect of theatre that almost everyone would include in a definition is this: *Theatre takes place in front of a live audience.* Shakespeare rather cannily refers to this using the words of the character of Hamlet: "Some must watch while some must sleep." If no one is watching the play, then it can be argued that the play actually didn't happen. The play isn't dead if there's no audience, but it is indeed sleeping. Theatre with no audience is a rehearsal at best. Someone offstage must witness the play to transform it from rehearsal into theatre. Again, as Hamlet says, some must watch.

So to sum up what might seem a simple question's very complex answer, we can only say this: Theatre is something that is defined less by the creators than it is by the audience. It is a live performance, which frequently tells a story—but not always—and it not only takes place in front of an audience, it *needs* to have an audience.

## introduction to the interview concept

The ways in which an "Introduction to Theatre" book can be written and structured are virtually limitless, and what constitutes vital information that must be imparted in such a book is the subject of an argument that could last until the end of time. In creating this text, the editor and authors have decided to focus on the "working" aspects of theatre: the careers and the people who bring plays to life for audiences. Using interviews with people who actively work in the field and teach techniques to students (who themselves desire to be working theatre professionals) seems like an effective way to truly "introduce" readers to the craft. The fact that the main author/editor of this book is a faculty member in an active theatre department provides a natural and geographically convenient cross-section of the industry to speak with. It is very important for students to know that these interviews express the ways in which *these specific individuals* have approached and do approach their work. All individuals in the field

---

2   Some of the greatest, most renowned playwrights, including Samuel Beckett, Eugene Ionesco, Kobo Abe, Antonin Artaud, Wilma Bonet, and literally hundreds of others, have created vibrant, effective, and exciting plays that follow no through line that fits the traditional definition of "a story." There are exceptions because, again, this is art.

3   The explosion of digital recording technology and the fact that the affordability and portability of this technology begs the question, "Yes, it is live, but can't I watch a recording of a live performance of a play?" The answer is yes, you can record and watch a live performance, but what you will be watching is in no way theatre. The direct human contact between the performers and audience cannot be recorded. Spoken words by the actors and laughter by the audience might come through with remarkable fidelity on your cell phone. But that is not what you experienced while the recorder was going. There are thousands of wonderfully produced films, videos, and digital recordings of live theatrical performances and they can be immensely moving to watch, but they are no more the true theatrical experience than an MP3 recording of a live music performance is the real experience of having seen that evening's concert.

have their own stories to tell. Given limitless time, we could talk to every person who does or has ever done theatrical work and get opinions and truths that contradict each other. It is important—vitally so—to stress that, while there are many similarities in the approaches taken by people all over the world to create theatre, there is indeed no definable "right" or "wrong" way. Ultimately, there is only the way that served *that specific play or production*. What worked creatively and technically for the Broadway opening night production of *Wicked* in 2003 might not work at all for the production of David Lindsay Abaire's *Good People*, set to open at the Cleveland Playhouse in March of 2013. However, it is not unlikely that there could be individuals who will end up getting work on both shows. Every show has its own needs, and every person in the industry has her or his own approach to addressing those needs. In this book, we let professionals talk to you directly through their interviews to give insight into how it is all done. Theatre ultimately is about choice, right or wrong, and for that reason a book introducing a reader to what theatre intrinsically is demands that choices be made. Because what is being discussed is an art form, the best anyone can do is say that this is generally how the experience works, while acknowledging that the variations, conflicting opinions, and idiosyncratic approaches of each theatre professional are valid. In short, if it works, it works, and this is how we, the authors of this text, have seen it work.

## what are the jobs of the theatre?

It is easy to underestimate what goes into producing a play, especially from a manpower point of view. For many people, the thought of making an actual living in the theatre is a foreign idea. Announcing to your parents, "I'm going to pay my bills in show business" is a statement that can terrify any student. The hesitance many feel about pursuing theatre as a life's work can be traced to the common misperception that the only employment available is on stage. The tendency can be to think that any show is really just the result of actors doing their best to perform in an entertaining and enlightening way. However, there are indeed myriad careers available to people who have the passion for the art. For each of the characters you see on stage on a given evening, there might be literally dozens of people who have worked on the project or are currently working behind the scenes as the performance goes on.

By definition, theatre is collaboration among many artists and technicians. It is created through the efforts of several individuals of differing skill sets, working together in harmony (hopefully) to make the show a success. In the world of theatre, both professional and amateur, a broad spectrum of expertise must be employed to put on an effective production. Among the more prominent jobs in theatre are: the producer, the director, the playwright, the actor, the stage manager, the dramaturge, the designers (set, costume, lighting, sound, makeup, props, special effects), the construction crew, the run crew, the house manager, the business staff (which includes box office sales/management, advertising/promotion, office management, financial administration, legal staff, public relations, and the all the ancillary jobs of running a business), and various technicians. Along with the previous list, you can add whatever people might be necessary to a specific theatre project, such as musicians, choreographers, fight choreographers, and vocal coaches. The theatre industry also includes thousands of teachers, from elementary school to the postgraduate programs that send trained aspiring professionals off into the working world. For instance, artists of great importance to the world of show business—such as Meryl Streep, Wendy Wasserstein, Lewis Black, David Allen Grier, Paul Newman, and Angela Bassett (to mention a few) all came through the training program at the Yale School of Drama, and Yale is just one of the more prominent names in the university world. The authors could list wonderful professional training programs for theatre professionals, not only from coast to coast in the United States (from the California Institute of the Arts School of Theatre in Valencia, California, to the University of Maine at Farmington) but across the world. Training theatre professionals, therefore, is an important job, creating an industry in itself.

There are also the construction, plumbing, electrical, and painting jobs that become available when a new theatre is built or an old one gets refurbished, and we aren't even mentioning the architects who have actually built the theatre. (At least not yet.)

Obviously, when thinking of all of these tasks that go into making a play work, you can see that there is a lot of opportunity for employment. Theatre is not just a craft or hobby or art; it is a genuine career path for thousands of people around the world. The major stagehands union in America, the International Alliance of Theatrical Stage Employees (IATSE), has over 113,000 members; Actors' Equity Association, the union which represents actors and stage managers, has over 49,000 members in the United States. There are also many theatrical artists who do sanctioned Non-Equity work for a living (albeit close to the vest) wage. So let's take apart what theatre professionals actually do.

h ow a play evolves from the mind of a playwright to a full production is a process that can take many different avenues. Among the writers and editors of this text are several playwrights who have had the privilege of seeing their work lived out upon the stage. Process is, in itself, a word that can create a lot of misperceptions; since writing for the theatre is neither a scientific formula nor a mathematical equation (although for some writers, perhaps it is), the idea of playwriting as a "process" might seem very technical. However, there *are* actual processes that are used to develop new plays. In this section, we will explore the development of a play, from the mind of the author to closing night, as it has been experienced by many writers, including the main author himself. Once again, it is vitally important to point out that this is in no way *the only way* a play can be developed. The writing process is intensely personal in any medium; theatre, poetry, novels, film, and even nonfiction. There is, to make an important point one more time, no right or wrong method to being a writer and creating work. In the final analysis, all that actually matters is that the development techniques give birth to a

# 1: the playwright and the play writing process

play that fulfills the author's desires from a storytelling and symbolic/message point of view. Whatever gets you there is just fine.

Here's a framework of how getting a new play polished and produced can, and often indeed does, happen.

First, there is the **Idea**. Something sparks in the mind of the writer that resonates as a story idea or an idea for a live theatre piece. The idea can be taken from anywhere: from popular culture, politics, religion, current events, or perhaps something much more personal to the author such as her or his relationships, upbringing, or personal difficulties or triumphs. Every play exists because, in the first analysis, the writer had an idea. This idea led to the next—and perhaps most important—step of the process: the **First Draft**.

The first draft. Writing is, in many ways, a very lonely experience. It isn't easy for a writer to get good work done if there are a lot of people around. (As I write this paragraph I am, in fact, sitting alone.) For most human beings who write, this solitary location is an absolute necessity. Of late, there are many who write in a coffee shop or in a park, which can work, but within that Starbucks or next to that serene lakefront the writer must find an environment that allows undistracted concentration to occur. It is the only way to get a draft done of any kind of work. The unfortunate fact is that this step, the first draft, is where most writing projects, especially plays, come to an end. Human nature being what it is, writers often succumb to two main threats: fear and laziness. You may ask, "What is there to fear?"

Everything.

*Playwright George Bernard Shaw*

The collection of "what ifs?" that face an author are endless because there are *endless ways in which the story can be expressed or the message conveyed.* Ultimately, an artist has to make choices; to "go with" certain ideas in the final analysis or the play can die right here in the first draft. Not every choice will be perfect. Not every choice will work. Some choices will actually be catastrophically bad, especially in the early drafts of a play. The fear that a good working version of the play will never coalesce can and often does paralyze the writer to the point that she or he simply doesn't write it, for fear that it will not be any good. This is a terrible shame, because no matter how bad the first draft may be, it can be fixed. It can be changed. A play is an elastic document.

If the writer pounds out a first draft that is utterly wretched, it's not necessarily a tragedy at all. Even that crummy first version has value, because it is *a viable starting point.* The writer can use that bad version as a template of *what not to do* in the next draft of the play. To all aspiring writers reading this text, here's the greatest advice you will ever receive: Finish that first draft! No matter what it is you are writing, finish it! You can go back and rewrite the parts that you feel have come out wrong. When it comes to art, there really aren't many (if any) "perfect" works. Leonardo da Vinci expressed this concept beautifully when he said, "I never *finish* a painting.

*Rewrite, rewrite, rewrite*

I only *abandon it.*" Writers all over the world will tell you that this is true. The first draft is vitally important to the playwriting process because it leads to the really hard work, which takes place in the next step, the **Rewrite Process**.

The rewrites (or second, third, fourth, et cetera, drafts) are just that. The author goes back to the pad or the keyboard and tries to improve the first draft. This part of the process is not only about fixing or eliminating flaws. It is also of great importance that the playwright keep what is good in the first draft going. A playwright must develop techniques—a craft, if you will—that lets them enhance and develop further those ideas in the nascent play that are succeeding. Simply put, you have to fully develop the stuff that works. A writer desires to mine all of the benefit she or he can out of those good ideas and take them as far as they can go creatively to tell the story and impart the message. Many writers will do something that is called "over-writing," which means taking the ideas that are sparking and creating a bulk of material with the intention of cutting the fat away at a later time. To use baseball as an analogy, it is better to have ten great pitchers in your bullpen and choose the most effective one for every situation that arises than it is to have just one good pitcher and hope he can do everything. A playwright stockpiles the good stuff because it simply isn't enough to fix or cut the flaws in the work. However there are likely to be plenty of flaws in a first draft, and this is the time for the writer to attack those flaws through reassembling words, shifting concepts, adding or subtracting characters, and maybe even nuking entire sections of the play.

The rewrite process in developing a play is, again, very personal. Some writers will do dozens of rewrites before showing the piece to a fellow artist or even a loved one. Some writers do not want to do too many drafts because they believe it makes the work stale or overthought. We find ourselves once more in the position of saying that there is no exactly defined perfect method that works for everyone, although there are many similarities among the various approaches taken by writers to cranking out the rewrites. Ultimately, if the piece has a future and is worthy of taking to the next step, the playwright reaches the stage that is often called the **Working Draft**.

The working draft is the version of the play that may not be ready to produce, but is ready to be shown to other writers and artists for criticism and input. Again, this is a very ticklish and dangerous place for the writer. It can be incredibly disheartening to be told that something you've worked on for quite a while, a play that you've sweated (and perhaps even cried) over is still not working. The outside eyes of trusted fellow artists and professionals can and often do make a huge difference at this point. Writers may have a cadre of professional theatre artists and fellow writers whom they trust to show their work when it's at this point. Perhaps they rely on just one personal reader/editor. Whatever works is once again the only rule. Most playwrights will confide to you that they are not worried that these people will hurt their feelings or not "like" their work. At this point, the author desires their person or cadre to give them useful, practical, and truthful input and suggestions. Practical suggestions are gold to a writer. The fact is this: It is just not enough to tell the writer that their play "doesn't work" or that it "stinks." That may well be, the working draft might be incomprehensible mush. But the writer needs to know *how* it is not working. *How* does it stink? What technical approach or implementable ideas can they suggest to get the work past its obstacles?

Becoming the confidant to a writer is a great responsibility and a marvelous opportunity. It is something the creators of this book hope happens to all of you, even if in reality you are just the confidant to your own taste. Anyone who teaches an Intro to Theatre course hopes that you, the reader/student, develop the same critical interpretive skills that a playwright looks for when they want input on their work. Every theatre professional craves informed theatregoers. You are the Audience, the consumers of art, and you deserve value for your time and money. As theatregoers, you can develop these critical skills fairly easily. All a person has to do is ask simple follow-up questions to their visceral reactions. If you like something, just ask yourself, "What specifically do I like? What did the artist/writer do that affected me? How did they do it?" If you think something stinks, ask yourself, "What were they trying to do? Why didn't it work for me? How could they have told their story or expressed their message more effectively?" You will quickly develop the ability to put your own taste into words. Understanding how the plays you

*A table reading*

see are created will be invaluable to you. You have the power to shape the art you see by becoming informed. This will also make you a more engaging person to talk to in social situations. The ability to delineate the "how" behind your opinions makes you an interesting person to seek for input. In the playwriting process, informed insights are invaluable to the author. An experienced outside eye helps the writer create directed and effective rewrites. If the input gathered by the playwright when she or he shows fellow artists and editors the working draft leads to positive growth of the script, the play might reach the next step, the **Table Reading**.

At a table reading, a playwright brings in actors to read and interpret the characters that have been created in the play. The table reading often is also attended by a director as well, and it is not unusual for that person to be the director if and when the script gets produced. At this junction, it is time for the writer to get off the page and out of her or his head. It's time to hear the words and the story. This first table read is quite frequently very informal. It is in no way unusual for the reading to be held at the writer's own home. The informality of this stage is partly because of budgetary reasons (no one wants to go rent an expensive theatre space to have their first listen of a play in development) and also because informality can lead to insight. In a completely relaxed atmosphere, the playwright can let her- or himself go and experience the piece. The first time a writer hears their words interpreted by talented performers can be a revelation. At this point, what is really cooking, what is really going well, pops out and excites the writer (at least this one.) It can be hard to believe that you wrote something that sounds so good because the actors take it to new and better places. Conversely, the parts that still are in need of repair, the sections that still aren't working (or maybe shouldn't even be there at all) clang loudly like a plumber's wrench hitting a brick wall. Despite what someone might think, hearing that clanging is heavenly. It means that what surrounds the nonworking section does indeed work. The writer can choose to rewrite the ineffective section or completely remove it. Perhaps the author can assign those words and ideas to a different character. The possibilities are myriad, and they open up in the writer's mind because the actors are bringing a new depth to the words. They are giving the words sound. Often at a table reading, playwrights will close their eyes and let their minds turn the spoken lines into pictures. They'll let the work present itself as a radio play. This kind of visualization can take authors out of their heads and puts them into the thoughts of the characters. From there, the needs, wants, and emotions of the characters come into focus. From the momentum gained in the first table reading, the playwright goes back into rewrites. If those rewrites go well, there are likely to be more table readings, and if *those* go well the project moves along to the next logical step, the **Staged Reading**.

A staged reading of a play often serves two functions. The artistic development of the piece is, of course, the first function, and the second function at this point is to showcase the script for potential producers. A staged reading ups the ante a bit. The show actually begins to move. Defined, a stage reading is a production of a play that uses actors to portray the roles with blocking while reading from the script. In many cases, there is an audience, and they may actually have paid for tickets to see the reading. A staged reading is a test of the play under laboratory conditions. It is time to show strangers and potential backers what the creation is becoming. Staged readings frequently include audience feedback through talkback sessions immediately after the reading, as well as written evaluations by the audience. The audience is given a reaction sheet and asked to give their opinion. These reaction sheets are precious. With the safety of anonymity, the people in the seats can be truthful to the point of brutality. This again might seem to be something the writer would dread, but in most cases it isn't. If the playwright's ideas are really taking shape and the story is being told coherently, there will not be too many major rip jobs in the evaluations. Those few

rip jobs will often contain some very useful input as well. It is important to read and digest all of the input the audience gives, from "That's wonderful!" to "What a monumental waste of ink!" and take whatever helps the piece from that information. The opinions of the audience, not only at a staged reading but anywhere along the line, are a gift. The playwright writes, the director directs, and the actors act because they want to stir the emotions of the audience. If the work doesn't make you react, good or bad, it is at best mediocre. As absurd as it may sound to the reader at this point, the staged reading usually leads to even more rewriting. There are small tweaks to be done. There may be sections that have slipped through that do not work on their feet, and those sections may have to be cut. Again, there are likely to be good things that should be taken even further in the script. It is in no way unusual for the staged reading to lead to other staged readings or perhaps table readings. The play is reaching a point of critical mass with regard to whether it will ever receive an actual production. It is risky for any theatre company or producer to put up a new work. Even if the writing and directing and acting and design aspects are done well, the show still could flop. Hard work, dedication, and talent guarantee nothing; it is art. Producing a play can bankrupt people. Show business is risky business. To get past this point, to get the play done onstage, the writer (as well as her or his agent or manager) has to look for backing and make pitches to theatres and investors. Many theatre companies offer new plays a forward step that mitigates the risk of full production, and a lot of very successful plays have been the beneficiary of this. That forward step is known as a **Workshop Production.**

The workshop production is a tremendous development tool for anyone who writes for the stage. All over the world, there are theatre companies that offer these productions to new plays. A workshop production is a fully acted, off book, directed presentation of a play. The design elements are usually minimal because the desire is to showcase the play while keeping costs to a bare minimum. Only those props, costumes, and set pieces that are completely necessary are used. The actors act the play for an audience full out; it is a real show, but it is scaled back.

If you are a fan of professional sports, think of it as a Minor League production. Many theatre companies, when they give workshop productions to new pieces, will present several of them in a festival setting. If you Google the phrase "new play festival," you will find dozens of examples. Workshop productions, like table and staged readings, quite often ask the audience to fill in a sheet with opinions, or are followed by talk-back sessions with the writer, director, and actors. This is an enormous opportunity for the creative team to hear the audience give their immediate input and gut reactions. Many plays have their ultimate creative breakthrough because of the questions and observations of workshop audiences.

A successful workshop production can lead, finally, to what the playwright has been hoping for ever since she or he had the initial idea. This final stage is, of course, the **Full Production**.

A full production of a play is just that—the play is produced with all of the aspects that the budget allows, such as lights, costumes, sound, music, full rehearsal, promotion, and a run of several weeks. A full production is very often reviewed in the local arts sections of the newspaper and maybe even on television or radio. The play, which was born out of the initial idea, gets a complete life and audience.

To conclude this section, it is once again prudent to note that many plays receive full productions without going through all of these stages or even any of them. In the end, once again, this is merely how many of his authors have experienced the play writing process. There remains no right or wrong way and there is indeed no road map. The point in theatre, from writing the play to acting the parts, all the way down to handing out the programs, is this:

Whatever gets you there, if it gets you there, is fine.

# cristina pippa, playwright interview

*WHAT INFORMATION DO YOU THINK AN "INTRO TO THEATRE" TEXTBOOK ABSOLUTELY MUST CONTAIN?*

I feel the most important thing is that theater is live. This makes it different than every other art form. It has been around since the beginning of man, and changes throughout history but it is always live. You can do it anywhere. All you need is at least one audience member watching and listening. Theater is live and collaborative.

*LIVE AND COLLABORATIVE ARE INTERESTING TERMS. COULD YOU DEFINE THEM FOR US?*

I usually start with the idea that all people, all human beings, are in some ways theatrical. You turn on a light or light a candle and you are doing lighting; you pick out a pair of jeans, you are costuming yourself; you speak in dialogue. Mamet says (paraphrased) "People don't always tell the truth but they do say something designed to get what they want."

*INTRO TO THEATRE BY NATURE FOCUSES ON THE ARISTOTLE STRUCTURE, THE WELL-MADE PLAY FORMAT OF PLAYWRITING. HOW MUCH DO YOU AGREE WITH THAT STRUCTURE AND WHERE HAS YOUR EXPERIENCE CAUSED YOU TO DISAGREE WITH IT? AS A PLAYWRIGHT DO YOU CONCERN YOURSELF WITH CONCEPTS LIKE EXPOSITORY SCENES, INTRODUCTION OF CONFLICT, CLIMAX, AND DENOUEMENT?*

To me that structure is a language we all speak in, straightforward speech has a beginning, middle and an end. If I am teaching Playwriting I tend to skip over [Aristotle Structure]. If you want to write the ending first, go ahead, at least in theatre. In Screenwriting it is more important to follow form and structure—you must have the inciting incident by page 10 or 12. In theater the writer doesn't necessarily have to do that. Lately there has been a precedent set against that structure. Back in the Sixties you would have naked people writhing or acting around you. There wasn't a need for structure. That is not to say that structure is wrong. [The character] Hedda Gabler has the feeling that something is wrong at the start and you do not necessarily know what it is. That has value. A play doesn't have to have structure but it must have conflict. All theater is based on conflict and all conflict is revealed through dialogue. What a young playwright sees as conflict is often boring not because of inauthenticity but lack of conflict. It is important that the playwright understand that conflict is vulnerability; not actual physical action. Characters must be emotionally vulnerable in order to create conflict.

*DESCRIBE IN YOUR OWN WORDS WHY THEATRE REMAINS A RELEVANT ART FORM IN THE 21ST CENTURY.*

Does it? Sometimes I worry about relevance. I personally struggle with this idea. I believe there are not enough productions of women's plays. I believe playwriting is relevant in the 21st century because it is live. We are sitting watching it live and watching the performers live so the risk is so much larger: if it doesn't work it is failing live in front of us. If it succeeds it succeeds live. Seeing *August Osage County* will always beat any movie I have seen as an experience because it was live.

*WHAT DOES THE WORD "CHOICE" MEAN TO YOU VIS-À-VIS THEATRE? HOW IMPORTANT IS THAT WORD TO YOU AS A THEATRE ARTIST?*

When I am talking to a producer about rewrites I know there is always a better choice. There are 80 million ways to write and produce a play. The writer has to pick one way and commit to it. Creating good work is less about the choices you ignore and more about the choices you make and stick with.

# how one play came to life

Tim Joyce

Making it through this process, from idea to full production, is something that this author has been lucky enough to experience a few times. How it happened was this: A show that I wrote called *Coffee On Wednesday* was given a workshop production several years ago by the Raven Theatre in Chicago. The play was performed three times on consecutive nights, a Monday, Tuesday, and Wednesday. Workshop productions often are performed on these so called "dark nights" of the week. It is a way to make efficient use of the theatre space since a workshop can be performed between weeks of the run of a full production using the set and lights from that piece. My workshop production in this instance occurred during such a stretch of dark nights. It was well received and attended. *Coffee On Wednesday* is a one-act play about two middle-aged friends who meet every Wednesday at the same diner. The play is a slice-of-life comedy about the challenges men face as they age and become aware that they no longer are young. Among its themes are infidelity, career disappointments, physical deterioration, and loss. Those themes might not immediately say "comedy" to the reader but they are in fact the backbone of humor. As the age-old saying goes: "Comedy is pain." As the author of a few comedic plays I can tell the reader that waiting to hear if the audience laughs at what you and the actors and director think is a funny line is an agonizing stretch of seconds. The workshop production of *Coffee On Wednesday* got those laughs (thank heaven!) all three nights. After the workshop shows were over I got a call from the artistic director of the Raven Theatre Company, Mike Menendian. He told me he really enjoyed the play and wanted to produce it the next year as a summer comedy. My initial idea had been rewarded. My play was going to get a full shot at a good theatre in a very big city. Mike had only one condition. He wanted the show to be full length. The running time of *Coffee On Wednesday* at the time was about 42 minutes. In order to call the show a full-length show we would have to come up with at least another 30 minutes of material. As a writer I knew that stretching the script of *Coffee On Wednesday* would probably hurt the piece. I was afraid it would end up being bloated. In several meetings Mike, as well as the director, Chuck Spencer, batted around ideas for how to make the show run long enough to be a complete evening of theatre. What was decided was that I would script another one-act play to be put up in tandem with *Coffee On Wednesday* and that this piece would take place in the same diner. I used many of the same characters and wrote the companion one-act, which is called *Without A Net*. A lot of care was taken that both one-acts be able to stand alone as stories. Together, those two plays were produced by Raven under the title *Diner Tales*." *Diner Tales* was well received and in fact received a Jeff Recommendation, which in the vibrant theatre community of Chicago is quite an honor. The story of this particular show, while very special to me, is not included here as an attempt to aggrandize myself or the people who created it. Many playwrights have had the good fortune to experience similar successes through the process (idea to first draft to working draft to table reading to staged reading to workshop production to full production) that has been described here. It is a long haul but it works.

ƒ rom the ground up, to get a play from the page to the stage, there has always been and always will be the question of money. It is true that the art of theatre does not in any way need to make a profit or have any kind of budget to create something significant and meaningful. A play can be performed in a subway station, a public park, a living room, or any other space where actors can assemble and an audience can watch. There's no guarantee that a big-budget show will be better than the show you see in the subway; good art happens wherever it happens. With that said, the fact remains that most theatre is dependent upon a budget of some kind. From renting space for rehearsal and performance to paying the salaries of the actors and staff, some form of financing is usually necessary.

Generally, professional theatre falls into two categories from a financial point of view: **For-Profit** and **Not-For-Profit**. The differences of approach are fairly accurately implied by the terms; For-profit theatre is created in the hopes of making money for investors, while not-for-profit theatre for the most part doesn't offer that potential. It is important to note, however, that the Not-for-Profits do, despite their name, attempt to run in the black; whatever monies

# 2: the producer

are earned by a particular production (or for that matter, whatever monies are earned over the course of an entire season of productions) are put back into the company rather than distributed to investors. This is not to say that in a not-for-profit situation the artists and staff are not making a living. Some of the most successful and prominent professional theatres in America and the entire world are run as not-for-profit corporations. In America, many of these institutions are members of the League of Resident Theatres (known in the theatre world as LORT for short.) Good examples of participating companies in the League of Resident Theatres include the Guthrie Theatre in Minneapolis; the Goodman Theatre in Chicago; the Seattle Rep; GeVa Theatre Center in Rochester, New York; the Berkeley Repertory Theatre in Berkeley, California; and the Lincoln Center in New York City. All in all, there are more than 70 professional not-for-profit theatre companies in LORT.

In either instance, for- or not-for-profit, the person or entity who is charged with the task of handling the financing of a play or a theatre company is called the **Producer**. The producer might simply be an individual who invests her or his money to finance a show. The producer might be the person who gathers several investors to share the cost of capitalizing the run of a play. The producer may, especially in the not-for-profit paradigm, be responsible for pursuing corporate, governmental, or private sponsorship and grant monies. At the high

*The London show* The Producers

end of the for-profit scale (such as Broadway), the producer is often not a specific person but a corporation or organization. Depending upon which source you use, the "average" budget for a Broadway production can be anywhere from $500,000 to $10 million. The wide range of costs to the producers can be attributed to many factors. Most notably, and simply, it is usually a lot more expensive to produce a musical than it is a "straight" play. The reason for this would be that the audience a Broadway producer wants to reach and attract for a musical has certain expectations that must be met for any given musical to compete with the other shows running on Broadway at the time. The musical theatre audience generally expects a lot of costumes, set changes, effects (both lighting and SFX, or special effects), as well as cast sizes large enough for the show to include major dance numbers. Recent shows have eclipsed those so-called average numbers ($500,000 to $10 million), and the costs will likely continue to rise. (According to the *New York Times*, two notably expensive shows, *Shrek, The Musical* and *Spider-Man*, cost $25 million and $75 million to produce, respectively.) Obviously, in the high stakes world of Broadway, the Producer is unlikely to be a single individual since the risk involved in the investment is so high. How high is that risk to investors? Again, there are many sources a person can cite, but according to both the Broadway League and the *New York Times*, only 20 to 30 percent of all productions in the Broadway District make back their original investment. In other words, 70 to 80 percent of Broadway shows lose money. It is high risk, indeed.

On the most basic level—the "storefront theatre" level—the producer might finance the play out of pocket. Across the United States and across the world, these "Storefront" companies and shows provide essential training grounds for theatre artists and technicians. These shows may not be able to pay the participants, but they provide crucial experience, a place to develop, and most significantly, an audience for new works and workers. What defines this type of theatre is not a question of quality necessarily; it is a question largely of budget and union participation. There are literally thousands of nonunion, non-Equity shows produced

*2008 Buffalo State College production of* Twelfth Night

all over the world every year in venues as small as living rooms and as large as cathedrals. All of these plays require someone to produce them, if only insofar as that producer finds the space where the performances take place.

The duties of a producer in theatre are not, however, totally fiduciary. Producers frequently are given a great deal of creative input, especially in the development of new plays, where they may even be responsible for suggesting changes to the script, such as cutting and adding scenes or

*The Pantages Theatre in Hollywood, CA*

songs or even entire plotlines and dialogue. Producers are often responsible for choosing the actors, directors, and designers who will create the production. An effective producer must have an eye for the art of theatre as well as the business. She or he has to be able to discern whether a given script is right for the theatre and its mission, not only financially but aesthetically. It is, in the final analysis, not an exaggeration to say that in the world of theatre, the show cannot go on unless the producer does her or his job.

# just what is broadway, really?

The Drifters had a huge hit in 1963 with a song that began with this lyric: "They say the neon lights are bright on Broadway" and George Benson had great success in the late 70's with it as well. Along with "Hollywood" that one word, "Broadway" is instantly recognized as meaning the top tier of entertainment and fame. Broadway is for a performer almost synonymous with Heaven; to be recognized there and work there means, especially to a stage Actor, that you have arrived and are at the peak of your craft. While this is a somewhat romantic vision it is to a certain extent true. Broadway is indeed where stage Actors and Directors and Playwrights hope to see their work presented. Attendance of Broadway shows in New York City routinely tops the 10 million mark every year, and the gross revenues of those shows is usually over $1 Billion annually. So you can see that Broadway is not only big prestige; it is very big business as well.

Historically theatre in New York City began with a handful of British theatre artists performing in the mid 1700's. The Revolutionary War slowed the progress of the Theatre Arts in New York, but shortly after, in 1798, a huge 2000 seat venue known as the Park Theatre opened and show business was off and running in Gotham. The original geographic location of New York's Theatre District was in Lower Manhattan, near the Bowery, but as the 19th Century progressed it migrated north towards Madison Square. After 1900 the northward migration of the District continued until, by the 1920's, the Broadway District we recognize today was geographically established in Midtown and centered around Times Square.

The distinction of being known as a Broadway Theatre or a Broadway Production is not simply geographic however. Due to the various pay scales and rights negotiations involved for theatre professionals, a fairly narrow definition of what "Broadway" is has evolved. To be considered a true Broadway show, the theatre space in which it is presented must have a seating capacity of at least 500. The theatre itself must be located in an area that extends from 40th Street to 54th Street, and from west of Sixth Avenue to east of Eighth Avenue, including Times Square.

Why make these distinctions? Again, simply, money. The amount that an Actor is paid, as determined by the Actors Equity Association, has graduated scales that are determined by location and designation of the Theatre where the show is mounted. "Scale", the lowest rate permissible to pay the performers on a weekly basis, is adjusted downward from Broadway (highest) to Off-Broadway (mid-level), to Off Off Broadway (the lowest union pay scale in New York City.) The Technicians, Directors, Stagehands, and Playwrights also are set into a pay scale that descends this way. These many factors explain why Broadway shows are the most expensive plays to produce, along with the need for marketing and advertising. Very few shows on The Great White Way come in under a budget of $5 million dollars, which explains why most shows there are not produced (as they commonly were in less pricey times) by individuals but rather by corporate theatre producing entities. Among these entities there are three main ones: Jujamcyn, the Nederlander Organization, and the Schubert Organization. Three Not-For-Profit companies fit the geographic and size recommendations for Broadway: The Lincoln Center Theatre, The Roundabout Theatre, and The Manhattan Theatre Club. These entities negotiate their contracts for productions with the League Of Resident Theatres (LORT) as opposed to working with the established producing organizations of commercial Broadway.

From an artistic/promotion standpoint it also makes sense for there to be geographic boundaries for what constitutes a Broadway Production. Allowing a show that is playing in the Bronx would devalue the meaning of Broadway, even though that production might be brilliantly written, directed, acted, and produced. Maintaining the integrity of what Broadway Theatre is defined as gives it a gravitas that can be marketed and promoted as something unique not only in New York City but the entire world. There is also the financial risk involved in producing a Broadway show (depending upon your source the number of productions that show a profit is between 25 and 35 percent) which demands that the Broadway distinction be protected as a brand name.

a running theme throughout this text is that theatre is about *choice*. This is what makes a production of a play happen, literally. A sentence in a play as simple as "I love you" presents an unlimited array of potential interpretations. The emphasis could be on the word "I"; the emphasis could be on "love"; the emphasis could be on "you." What the sentence means to the character speaking it, the character it is being spoken to, and the play in general, comes down to trying various approaches and making the best selection from all the approaches that have been explored. For an Actor this presents a challenge that for the most part he/she cannot face alone. The choices made by the Actors need an Outside Eye, and that Outside Eye is the Director. Ultimately the Director chooses what ideas are going to be a part of the performance.

Helping Actors with choices during rehearsal (or in some cases actually making choices for them) is a significant part of the Director's job, but it is far from the main task the director faces and is entrusted with. A Director usually comes into Production with a concept; an approach to the text and the execution of that text onstage that she or he believes will make the entire production coher-

# 3: the director

ent. Even in the lightest of comedies, where the audience might believe that the Director's only assignment is to make sure the laughs are there, there is more often than not a *message and a theme*. Very often a play has a specific political or sociological point of view which the Director wants to bring out in the production. At the first Production Meeting, where all of the creative staff excepting the Actors meet to talk about how the play is going to be presented, the Director is generally the main voice, she or he explains the concepts that they desire for the production, vis-a-vis technical, artistic, and message/theme elements. In most theatrical situations, the Director has the final say on all of these. The goal of any production of a play is to create beautiful art through collaboration of course, but somebody has to make the final decisions about its production choices, and that is the responsibility of the Director.

By that first Production Meeting most Directors have read the play so many times that they could recite every line if asked. It is a huge part of the Director's job to do this reading. The Director has to understand the significance of every line, every moment, and every action that the play presents; and then have the ability to bring it all together through the rehearsal process. And by rehearsal process we are not talking only about the work that is done with the Actors, we are also speaking about the technical and practical aesthetics. A Director has to not only know what each character says in a scene, but *why* the characters

*Director Mike Nichols*

say what they say and for that matter why the scene was written into the play by the Playwright in the first place. The Director also has to be brutally honest about the weak points that may exist in the text, as well as the limitations of the Actors in the cast. No artist is purely perfect; some of the writing might (even in a renowned and respected play) be clumsy or outdated, and the Director might be called upon to make cuts in the script to fix those weaker moments. (This is especially true when directing a Shakespeare play or any play that is from an era where language was significantly different. Some of the contemporary references in a play by legends like Shakespeare or Moliere or Euripides are now very far from contemporary; a political scandal and the names associated with it from the year 400 B.C. needed no explanation then, but now it might need to be explained or cut. On top of all of this, there is the question of running time. Modern audiences are not very patient about sitting too long in any one place, and the general attention span these days makes it hard to have a financially successful show that runs for more than two or two and a half hours.) Part of the Director's job is therefore editing as well as interpreting.

As we stated in the last paragraph, the limitations of the Actors with regard to their ability to portray their roles is also a challenge any director will tell you is a major aspect of their task. In a Broadway show the Director might find her/himself with a "Star" performer whose name will indeed sell tickets, but whose ability to play the part might not be ideal. In these cases the Director needs to make adjustments to compensate for the weaknesses while simultaneously bringing the best out of the Actor's talent. An effective Director doesn't just fix what is bad, she/he also enhances and explores what is good. Sometimes the challenge is the opposite from being handed a Star to Direct. Often the person who ultimately gets cast was not the first (or even the second, third, or fourth) choice for the job. In a University setting, the Director is more often than not also one of the instructors in the department. In these cases their responsibility is not only to cast the best actor for the role, but occasionally to throw a part at a young Actor that stretches or challenges them to become a more complete artist.

To bring a play from the script to the actual performance of that script is a daunting task indeed. Most Directors work, through rehearsal, with the general paradigm being that the play will be broken down into smaller pieces, worked on for shape, message, and effective telling of the story, and then reconstructed (again in rehearsal) as a total work of art. Since the preponderance of plays are performed in two Acts, the majority of Directors will work these acts separately and then join them. But the sectioning off of the text for rehearsal purposes goes much deeper than that. Each moment must be rehearsed, analyzed, staged, and made into a polished section that incorporates into the whole. Think of this as the same process an artist goes through when she/he creates a glass

*2009 Buffalo State College production of* In The Blood

*The Bolshoi Theater of the USSR*

mosaic: every tiny piece of the picture is shaped, colored, polished, and perfected to the best of the abilities of the artist. These tiny pieces are then connected to create the full picture; but the process does not end there. The edges, the blending of spaces and the smoothing over that needs to be done to hide the seams, is no small part of the undertaking. The individual polished pieces must fit back together to create a coherent Whole.

That is, generally, how a director creates a production of a play through rehearsal. Let us look at the mechanics of it.

There is a common term in the theatre, especially in America, that is used by many (but once again we must add the caveat: "Not All") Directors and it is called a **Beat**. (This is also known by many stage artists as a **Moment**.) A Beat is an individual section of the script that contains an emotional transaction between characters or within one character. It can be One Line; One word; One Action; or Several Lines. These Beats are the smallest parts of the play: they are the atoms from which the organism is created. A Beat can be as simple as one character saying "I hate you" and another character reacting to that sentence. It could be something non-verbal, like a character taking a rose from a vase and throwing it into a garbage bin. What makes a Beat or a Moment in a scene is this: Emotion is shared or traded or reacted to onstage. That traded/shared/imposed emotion then demands a reaction from the characters or character who've experienced the Beat. It can be shared, this emotional exchange, by as many characters as are standing onstage at that Beat; or it can be something emotional, a transitional reaction, that is experienced by only one person on the stage as they stand there alone within the scene. In a rehearsal of an individual scene, a Director may ask her/his Actors to try an individual Beat many different ways. When the aforementioned character says "I hate you" the first choice of the actor speaking the line may be to scream it. But, when you think about it, the character might gain even more power and emphasis from simply saying the line in a normal tone of voice with a smile. The reaction of the character to whom this line is spoken may actually be the person upon whom the Director wants the audience to focus. If the reader allows themselves to think of this kind of *emotional transaction* as it has happened in her or his life they might think about how devastating a quiet sentence can be. The most powerful moments, emotionally, in our lives are not necessarily screamed at us. Sentences that change the lives of real people (and therefore the

*2009 Buffalo State production of* The Grapes of Wrath

sentences that make the most powerful dialog) in the most profound ways are often spoken to us in the most oblique fashion. "You're hired." "We have to let you go." "I'm afraid she passed away."

These are among the sentences that profoundly shape our lives, and often we receive these Moments, these emotional transactions, in very few words and with finely parsed emotion.

That is not to say that the smaller, less dramatic or emphatic reading of a line is always the best choice or even the most common choice arrived at in the communication between a Director and Actor. Sometimes those dramatic moments are indeed shouted to the rafters. What is important, when functioning as the Director of a play, is to explore *as many possible choices* given the rehearsal time allotted, and then to build from the best choices that mosaic that becomes the entire play.

Rip it apart. Polish it. Put it back together and smooth over the gaps. That is a large part of the job for any Director.

Then there are the technical aspects to Directing, the craft that must go with the art. The Director is the person who **blocks** the play. Blocking is, in its simplest definition, telling the Actors where to stand and what movements to make on stage. However there is a great deal more involved to effectively blocking a play than simply making sure the Actors do not slam into or obstruct each other onstage. Some Directors approach blocking casually in rehearsal; allowing the Actors to explore the space and make the moves that organically happen. On the other hand there are Directors who will arrive at the first rehearsal with the entire play blocked. The latter is unusual these days because Actors tend to bristle at this approach, but in situations such as Summer Stock theatre, where a play might only rehearse for five days before opening, it does happen.

So why is blocking important in the first place? Why does a Director need to control or instruct the Actors about their movement on the stage? There are a lot of reasons why, and the foremost is this: During a play, there are those multitudinous Beats/Moments where it is crucial that the eyes of the audience are focused on the essential action. Not every character onstage is at any given moment the focus of the scene. If an Actor who is *not* the focus of the scene or the Beat/Moment is drawing the eyes of the people in the seats to her or him, it hurts the play. (And it really can annoy the Actor who IS supposed to have focus…) Everyone knows the term "Upstaging" whether they are in the theatre or not. When we are upstaged in real life, someone steals the attention that is rightfully ours. This is why the dresses worn by the Bridesmaids are never as beautiful as the gown worn by the Bride. We, the guests at the wedding, are supposed to be focused on HER. In real life this can be a cause of tension, but onstage it can ruin a production of a play. A Director needs not only to know who should be in focus but how to put that character there; hence we have blocking. Generally speaking the area of the stage toward the back wall, the Upstage Area, draws focus because the Actors who are speaking to the characters upstage have to turn their faces away from the audience to make eye contact. That's why Upstaging is called that. A selfish Actor can sneak upstage and force their scene partner/partners to give them focus. However Upstage isn't the only place a Director can send an Actor to find focus. The lip of the stage, the point closest to the audience, also has its power. This is as far Downstage as the character can go, and that proximity to those watching the show has the potential for great emotional effect inherent in it as well. Human beings also tend to look toward the center of things, so Center Stage has its gravitas as well when it comes to drawing focus. And finally there is the question of movement. If an Actor who is not supposed to be in focus moves while everyone else stands still, they take focus. The human eye reacts to movement, a biological fact that came in handy long ago when there were Sabre Toothed Tigers in the neighborhood. On top of all of this most Directors desire the placement of Actors onstage to create an overall aesthetic; they want the stage picture to be pretty (or dynamic or interesting) and use the staging of the Actors in much the same way as painters do when placing their subjects on a canvas. Blocking, therefore, is one place where the art and the craft of the Director juxtapose.

To sum, the Director, when blocking, wants to allow the Actors to explore the space and how their characters move within it while at the same time correcting the focus of the scene as well as the overall aesthetic beauty of the stage picture.

Directors must work with a variety of personalities. Some Designers are easier to work with than others. Some Producers are more hands on than others. With a new play it is entirely possible that the Director is working along with the Playwright during the Production process.

And then there are the Actors. Acting is a strange beast, and the people who pursue it need to have a lot of qualities in order to succeed. What makes Acting strange is that many of the qualities necessary to do it well work against each other within the average human psyche. The best Actors bring a vulnerability to their characters. They are often open vessels that can take on multiple personalities and voices. They need to be open to their emotional pain and willing to explore it creatively. At the same time they have to own a skin thick enough to be rejected at dozens of auditions without giving up. They have to be able to overcome the fear of failing in front of a large room full of strangers. What all of this means is that Actors can be very temperamental: very relaxed, very tense, or any combination of these traits. They can be quite complex to work with. The Director needs to get the most out of member of the cast and that requires some psychology. It is like managing a baseball team: some people are effectively motivated by a kick in the rear end, and some people are motivated by a pat on the back. Any

Baseball Manager or Theatre Director will tell you that kicking the butt of the person who needs a pat on the back can be disastrous. Furthermore the Director is working within a time frame that demands constant progress during rehearsal, and ultimately is hoping that the entire cast becomes a cohesive unit that can simply be called The Show.

Throughout rehearsal the Director is setting up the individual Moments and Beats of the play. Getting the entire cast on the same page, getting them to exist within the world of the play, requires breaking the script down into pieces. These pieces are rehearsed, discussed, adjusted, and occasionally argued over during the rehearsal period. All the while, as the Director is creating these small pieces of the performance, she or he has to keep an eye on the overall concept. The Director needs those pieces, when put back together, to be a tapestry that tells the story within the theme of the play and delivers the message the entire production intends. Again we are talking both Craft and Art occurring simultaneously, with perhaps just a bit of Alchemy thrown in.

# two directors talk about directing, acting, and teaching acting

'

The authors of this book were fortunate enough to be in constant contact with a variety of theatre professionals. Among them were two, Donn Youngstrom and Drew Kahn, who bring many unique perspectives to the task of Directing a play. Both men are accomplished Directors and Actors with extensive experience, and both have taught students for many years on a college level about Directing and Acting. Here are some of their insights.

*DREW KAHN, WHEN ASKED ABOUT THE TASK OF DIRECTING A SCRIPT, MADE THIS FASCINATING OBSERVATION:*

When I'm Directing I don't start with the play. At first I see my task as building a world, a community within the cast. I even use words like **sacred** for the environment in which the actors will rehearse. An actor has to consider their work sacred, and this is often hard for a young actor. The teacher must define what that means. It is not about being a star, making a great deal of money, or even the competition that is inherent in getting the role. A young actor has to have to have a shift in their thinking to become the artist they can truly be. They have to do the unthinkable. Which indeed is to think of yourself as an artist. An actor, in order to do their best work, must attack the craft full throttle, with commitment, no fear, and no judgment. I tell the actors I Direct and the actors in my classes that you must have the courage to see yourself, as you truly are. For this reason, both in the rehearsal of a play and in my Acting classes, I strive to create an environment where all things are possible.

*DONN YOUNGSTROM EXPRESSED THIS IDEA OF THE "WORLD OF THE PLAY" WITHIN HIS OWN IDIOM, AND THESE WERE HIS OBSERVATIONS ON THE DIRECTOR'S JOB:*

One of the hardest things for a director is creating that "World of the Play." Where is this world? Is everyone in the cast in the same world? I find this especially important in Shakespeare. Directing Julius Caesar was my Master of Fine Arts Thesis at Brooklyn College. My production took place in a Black Box theatre with very low ceilings. So, rather than going with an Elizabethan look or togas, we took the production and set it in 3rd World Latin America. Rather than wearing Khaki we differentiated the character of *Julius Caesar* by dressing him in white. This white costume created a challenge for the Costume Designer, which was this: given the murder of Caesar through multiple stab wounds, how, given his white costume would we deal with portraying the bloodiness of that scene? This Costume Designer quite ingeniously suggested that we give all the senators red sashes, and after they stabbed Julius Caesar they each laid their ribbons down by the body. Brutus, then tries to keep the assassination ceremonial, a ritual of violent political coup rather than simple murder or slaughter. It was a profound effect and it provided the production with  a moment that was evocative of the traditions of Asian Theatre. The effect looked like blood "coming off" the corpse. I've always credited the Costume Designer for that. A Director must collaborate, must be open to the ideas of other members of the production. If an actor comes up with a great idea, take it and give credit where it is due. The success of the play is more important than the ego of any of the artists. I get lots of compliments on my blocking, but a lot of it is letting the actors follow their movement instincts. If an actor starts to fidget I ask

"Do you want to move?" Usually they say yes, and so then I say go ahead. Eventually of course I have to fix the stage picture, but I use the movements and placements of the Actors as much as I can. I want the stage picture to benefit from and reflect the instincts of the Actors.

*ASIDE FROM CREATING THAT "WORLD OF THE PLAY" I'M THE SAFETY NET ALLOWING THEM TO HAVE FUN, TAKE CHANCES, TAKE ARTISTIC RISKS, AND ULTIMATELY I HELP THEM GET UP WHEN THEY FALL.*

I often think about this quote by Jonathan Miller, who among many accomplishments Directed Christopher Plummer in his acclaimed performance as the title character in Shakespeare's "King Lear":

"The Director is, in short, the creator of intuitive insights at moments where rehearsal might otherwise grind to a halt."

† heatre has a very direct point of contact, and that contact is the Actor.[1] The words of the Playwright, the concept and interpretation of the Director, and the inspiration and craft of the Designers are all a very essential part of a successful theatrical production; but the moment of communication, the sharing and emotional bond that a play forges with an audience ultimately falls into the Actors' hands. A play consists of Moments[2], sections of time on stage where the cast and those who watch are experiencing a world that only exists at that place and during that exact temporal reality. Feelings, action, message, and the very art that is a well-produced play, are all shared in these Moments between the audience and the performer. The Actor's job is complex. The Actor's job is simple. The simple task is to play a Character, to bring a part in the play to life onstage. The complex job is those aforementioned simple things, as well as becoming an artist whose work can be recreated every night without losing the core of the character and while effectively reaching the audience with their body as well as their voice and emotion. An Intro to Theatre student may think to her/himself that the most challenging aspect is learning the lines and the blocking. Those things are important of course, but they represent a tiny

# 4: the actor

part of the actual task that an Actor faces in bringing life to a role. Creating a Character is infinitely more complex than remembering words and cues in order and avoiding tripping over the furniture. By the time a show opens the Actor has probably read their part more than a thousand times, not so much for memory but for interpretation. The Actor reads, rereads, re-rereads, and then reads the script some more---looking for the things she or he will use to be effective. By the time Opening Night rolls around there've been weeks or even months of rehearsal so half the blocking by opening night is simple muscle memory. This Character, this Role in the play, should seem to the audience to be a living, breathing, real, and believable human being who is experiencing everything that the Character is going through. If the Character is Ophelia in Shakespeare's "Hamlet" experiencing a descent into suicidal madness through grief for her father, then the Actor playing the part has to invite the audience into a world where that is truly happening. The sad song that Ophelia sings with its imagery of flowers and loss must be a Moment where the audience is connected and emotionally moved. Simultaneously that actor has to speak

---

1   In modern theatre the word "Actor" is considered genderless. Women and Men are both referred to as Actors.

2   "Moments" within a play are also commonly referred to as "Beats." The fact is that there are many ways to describe these small emotional segments, and many Directors and Actors have their own idiosyncratic terms for them.

*John Barrymore in* Hamlet

clearly, move with grace and purpose, react to the other Characters, and ultimately leave those in the seats observing convinced they've seen a beautiful emerging young woman in the throes of emotional distress that will leave her deceased soon.

Making that moment, which is just one moment by one Character in a complex play with myriad moments and several principal Characters, work as it should, underscores the task and challenge of being a truly good Actor.

Here's an overview of the basic skills a proficient Actor should possess.

Actors must train themselves to truly listen to the other Actors. This is very hard to do. In day to day conversation most of us would admit that more than half the time we are waiting for a gap in our friend's story where we can jump in and say what we want. Without listening between the Actors onstage, theatre can become very predictable and boring. A non-listening Actor is throwing away the gifts the other Actors are handing out, which is new insight and development of the scene and the play. This need to become an accomplished listener is why every basic acting course a person will ever take starts with the Instructor uttering this sentence: "Acting is Reacting."

It is absolutely the best advice any actor ever gets.

But there are many other facets an Actor wants to have and develop.

Actors need to be accomplished at reading and interpreting a text. They have to be able to take not only their lines and understand them intrinsically, they also must know the meaning and import of all the words contained in the play. So an Actor must be an insightful reader to be fully effective.

Actors must develop and be able to effectively use their body as an interpretive tool. An Actors' body is her/his Instrument, along with their Voice. With regard to use of the body an Actor needs to be able to inhabit a person, "The Character," in a physical way that shows the audience who this concocted human being is through movement. Actors often find themselves playing a character who is older or younger than they are in real life, so it is essential to know how to control and transform their body into the person the play needs them to be. Whether it is the grotesque hunchback of Richard III or the electrically seductive/simultaneously brutal presence of Stanley Kowalski in "A Streetcar Named Desire" an Actor has to be able to bring their body along in the process of Character creation and use movement to give the role life. Actors often spend hours watching people in public, looking at how they walk, how they use their hands, how they present their energy through posture to those around them. Laurence Olivier (A name that is almost always mentioned when the question "Who is the greatest actor ever?" comes up at a party) often used animals as models when creating a role. He'd take on the posture of an ostrich or a wolf perhaps, and base his movement in rehearsal on that animal. Olivier's process included picking an animal that he believed was like the Character he was chosen to play. Using the physical traits

*2006 Buffalo State production of* The Diary of Anne Frank

of that beast as a metaphorical base he'd create a new person, a version of himself who was not himself, and bring that hybrid physical presence to the performance.

Actors must develop their voice, to learn to see their vocal chords as an Instrument through which they project their lines and the feelings those lines contain and convey, and use that developed voice with effect and clarity. "Instrument" is not a pretentious term here; it is the word which Actors actually use to describe their Voice and Body, and it is not at all an inaccurate metaphor. A woman playing the role of Medea, in order to bring the Character to life as well as to do justice to the spectacular poetry of the Playwright Euripides, must be able to control her voice, to play melodic scales with inflection, volume, rhythm, and varying speed of delivery such that an audience not only is enthralled but understands the complexity of the language. That is a good definition of what a musician does with her instrument. She masters it, whether it is a trombone or a guitar or an accordion, so she can evoke every last bit of emotion and melody from it whenever she desires, and bring all of that to whatever the needs of the song are. An Actor must have an effective and well developed vocal instrument so she/he can do justice to ANY role they might be fortunate enough to find themselves hired to portray.

Development of the Vocal and Physical (Movement) Instrument for most Actors is a lifelong job and many of the greatest stage Actors, as well as those who aspire to that greatness, continue working in Voice and Movement classes as well as with private coaches and teachers for their entire lives to keep their instrument[s] in working order.

So that is the story behind the Actors' Instruments. But what about the actual creation of a Character as a living emotional being? How do Actors do that?

There are many schools of acting, and the number of techniques that have been developed throughout the centuries is formidable. We come up once again to the point that permeates this entire text: Theatre is an ART and therefore no single approach is necessarily right or wrong. Theories abound about how to create a Character, and they have been written about for a very long time. Different schools of Acting tend to fall into two main subgroups in their approach: INSIDE/OUT or OUTSIDE/IN.

To explain what this means and the differences in the approaches are let's go to the heart of what an Actor hopes to accomplish when she or he is cast in a role. The Actor wants that role to be interesting, exciting, emotionally engaging, dynamic, and most of all believable to the audience. The Actor wants a Character whose authenticity and commitment is never questioned by those who are watching. They want the audience to think they are actually the person they are portraying. In order to get that level of commitment and belief from those who bought tickets to see the performance the Actor must be alive and in the moment during the entire play. An Actor must have a believable emotional core. The quest for that emotional core, that place within the Actor that makes an audience certain that the Actor truly feels the emotions the Character is experiencing, is where the divergence between Inside/Out and Outside/In becomes relevant.

Going back to our use of Sir Laurence Olivier as an example, we can see the Outside/In approach in action. Olivier tried to find the **Body**, the **Movement** that defined his Character first. Using the words of the script and the new form of his body that he had created, Olivier, through the rehearsal process, would allow his emotional core to develop. Olivier also was a master of his Vocal Instrument; he chose the way his characters would sound and played with that sound during rehearsal like a brilliant jazz musician. In the final analysis Olivier trusted that, by moving his body in his Character's own idiosyncratic way, and speaking the lines beautifully and truthfully to the other Characters on stage (while truly listening to what they were saying as well) his inner emotional core would develop and come alive. This technique worked well enough for him to become a legend. Many Actors throughout time and to this day work this way. Sometimes this is referred to as "Technical" Acting; but that term is unnecessarily pejorative. It implies that an Outside/In Actor doesn't play a living Character but just sounds and moves like one. That is far from the truth. The final destination of an Outside/In Actor, if done effectively, is the same place arrived at by a skilled Actor working Inside/Out; that is to say, both techniques can lead to a living, breathing, complex and believable Character.

Following is a quote from Olivier himself, speaking in an interview during the 1960's in the book "Great Acting"[3] which was a series of interviews with legendary stage performers compiled by Hal Burton. In speaking about the concept of **OUTSIDE/IN**, Burton asks Olivier to talk about the process that led him to his iconic characterization of the title role in Shakespeare's "Richard the Third" at the Old Vic Theatre in London; a portrayal that, in the opinion of many critics, directors, and fellow actors of his generation cemented him as the greatest Classical stage actor of his era:

> "I thought about [Walt Disney's animated] physiognomy of the Big Bad Wolf, which was said to have been founded upon Jed Harris [A New York Stage director who Olivier actually hated.] Hence the nose I used, [based on Disney's Big Bad Wolf] which originally, in the sketches, was very much bigger than it finally was in the film. And so with one or two extraneous externals, I began to build up a **character—a characterization**. I usually collect a lot of [external] details, a lot of characteristics, and find a creature swimming about somewhere in the middle of them."

---

3   Refer to Page 24 In The Director Chapter.

So just what does it mean to say that an Actor is working Inside/Out? A little bit of history is absolutely necessary here. Inside/Out Acting has been around a long time. There are anecdotes about Greek actors who went to immense lengths to feel the feelings of their characters, up to and including stories of Actors who actually physically attacked other Actors and stagehands during performances. The ascendancy of modern Inside/Out Acting however, is generally accepted to have begun with the work of Konstantin Stanislavsky. Stanislavsky was an Actor and Director who worked with the legendary playwright Anton Chekhov at the Moscow Art Theatre in the late 19th Century. Stanislavsky, through his seminal books *"An Actor Prepares"*, *"An Actor's Work on a Role"*, and his autobiography, *"My Life In Art"* described his, and his Russian theatre contemporaries, search for a style of acting that would create "Theatrical Truth." This revolution in approach to Acting led to the rise of The Group Theatre in New York, where great Teacher/Actor/Directors such as Lee Strasberg, Stella Adler, and Sanford Meisner developed techniques meant to create realism onstage through an approach to acting that generally became known as "The Method."

Method Acting deserves its own book, and in fact there are thousands of them. To very briefly on a surface level summarize The Method, and Inside/Out Acting, one would say that it involves an approach where the Actor searches to create a role by feeling the actual emotions of his/her Character from the very first, at the time they are cast in the role. Then, through rehearsal, a Method Actor aspires to create her/his role using the feelings that are at their personal emotional core to build the Character into a fully realized human being onstage. The emphasis is on finding the psychological and emotional history and influences of the Character. Strasberg used a technique that came to be known as "Sense Memory" (also referred to as "Affective Memory" or "Gestalt") with his students: he'd encourage his Actors, at crucial emotional points of a play, to think about the times in their personal lives when they felt the way their character was feeling. For example, if an Actor is playing Ophelia, who has just found out that her father has been murdered by her lover, that Actor would strive to find a memory from their own life that was similarly painful. Perhaps the Actor lost her mother in a car wreck when she was young. She'd then use that awful painful memory as an emotional launching point when grieving her father as Ophelia onstage. Sense Memory work tends to be very intense and it takes a lot of courage and commitment to use your own pain in that fashion. On the subject of Sense Memory Sanford Meisner wholeheartedly disagreed with Strasberg. Meisner believed that, if an Actor was remembering her/his personal emotions during the powerful moments in a play, they weren't truly in Character; instead they were displaying their real life feelings. Meisner argued that the Actor should focus on the "Given Circumstances" of the scene and then invest their emotions as intensely as they could towards the other Characters. This he believed would lead them to react with pure emotional honesty to the scene that was occurring. In short Meisner felt that, if the Actor truly believed she/he was **actually experiencing the moment in real time** they would feel real emotions and be perfectly emotionally genuine onstage. Meisner referred to this as "living truthfully under imaginary circumstances."[4] Stella Adler branched off, calling her years with the Group "the worst of my theatrical life" and taught a synthesis of styles. Interestingly, Adler was coached by Stanislavsky himself while she was in rehearsals for the Group Theatre's Broadway Production of Howard Lawson's play "Gentlewoman." In these coaching sessions, which created great controversy within the company, the great Russian artist himself apparently

---

4   Once again "Acting is Reacting."

repudiated some of the concepts most cherished by acolytes of The Method, most notably Strasberg. Addressing Adler's discomfort with the use of *"affective [sense] memory"* in her portrayal, Stanislavsky is reputed to have said to her "If my system doesn't help you, don't use it." The translator present at this exchange, a native French speaker as it turns out, asserts that he told her that his "System Exercises" were a last resort for an actor suffering a creative block; not a method for rehearsal or training. This is a controversial conversation and seems to run contrary to what Stanislavsky actually wrote in the text of "An Actor Prepares" in which an entire chapter is devoted to "sense (or affective) memory."

The veracity of this exchange remains controversial, and both Strasberg and Adler never really settled the rift that arose from her departure from the ideals espoused by her fellow Group member. A great deal of writing exists about this rift, especially since Adler went on to say that her input from the Russian Master could be described as an endorsement of "starting from the outside." Those four words to Lee Strasberg were simply heresy.[5]

It is important at this point to discuss the idea of the theatre space itself. Where a play is being performed affects those performing it and their stylistic choices. If, for instance, an actor finds herself playing Viola in Shakespeare's "Twelfth Night" with one of the numerous outdoor festivals across the world such as Shakespeare in the Park in Central Park, that will influence the style of her performance. Outdoor theatres sometime have crowds well into the thousands, and the view of those audience members at the "top of the hill" is quite different than what the early birds at the stage's edge are seeing. Outdoor acting is, for lack of a prettier term, "Bigger" or "Declamatory." In order to effectively convey the humor or suffering within a play to people far away requires more sweeping and stylistic movement. This obviously puts the Actor at loggerheads with the concept of any kind of "pure" realism: in real life we don't walk through rooms with sweeping arcs or talk indoors at high decibel levels. (At least hopefully the reader doesn't yell in his/her living room…) Again, the caveat that must permeate this text comes into play; this is art. There is no right or wrong. There is only that which is effective or ineffective, and even those standards can be debated endlessly. Ironically, given that so much modern outdoor theatre is his work, Shakespeare and his fellow actors performed their plays in a very intimate space. The Globe Theatre was not a sweeping opera house with thousands of seats, it was a comparatively small venue and in fact the Groundlings were close enough to the stage to get sprayed with spit when the actors were popping their consonants. Shakespeare and his company, The Lord Chamberlain's Men (later changed to The King's Men when Charles the First replaced Queen Elizabeth the First), had to use a great deal of subtlety in their acting and a lot of this was due to the space. Through Hamlet's instruction to the actors we hear the Bard himself speak out about this:

> HAMLET: Speak the speech, I pray you, as I pronounced it to you, trippingly on the tongue. But if you mouth it, as many of our players do, I had as lief the town crier spoke my lines. Nor do not saw the air too much with your hand, thus, but use all gently, for in the very torrent, tempest, and (as I may say) whirlwind of your passion, you must acquire and beget a temperance that may give it smoothness. O, it offends me to the soul to hear a robustious periwig-pated fellow tear a passion to tatters, to

---

5   University of Birmingham (Uk) College of Arts and Law Press: "The American Evolution"

very rags, to split the ears of the groundlings, who for the most part are capable of nothing but inexplicable dumb shows and noise.

Shakespeare obviously had a very strong opinion on what defined good or bad acting. His advice is subtlety: "don't saw the air with your hands and weep and wail with false passion" is his point. The Globe, and later the very compact space of the Covent Garden in London, demanded finesse rather than bulldozing from its actors. This need to address the space and adapt your performance to it is another of the skills required and expected of an effective Actor. He or she must reach each member of the audience to the best of their ability. Outside/In or Inside/Out is part of the choice along with the needs of the play and the desires and concept of the director.

Finally, and for theatre professionals and amateurs alike this is a great part of why people fall in love with the theatre, the argument as to which approach to Acting, Inside/Out or Outside/In, is more artistically legitimate, more pure, or better art, has kept many Directors, Playwrights, Actors, and Critics arguing until well past Closing Time for decades. In the USA during the latter half of the 20th Century it was almost heretical to argue in favor of approaching a role from the Outside In. The reality is this: neither approach is ever likely to entirely disappear from Acting. The competition for roles, along with the need for an Actor to be flexible enough to work in limitless genres and spaces and even languages with a myriad of Directors in plays that range from pure reality to wordless avant-garde scripts, demands that a working Actor be able to function in many realities. Most Actors are not 100% Outside/In or Inside/Out; they study as many approaches as they can and take what works *for them* to create their own personal Method. The techniques, for an Actor, are the All-You-Can-Eat Buffet; and the smart Actor only chooses to put what they really want, what is most nutritious to them, on their plate.

† heatre asks a great deal from those who create it. The director, the actor, the playwright, and all of the designers not only have to work within a budget and an all-too-often tight timeframe, but they also are expected to all come together with a vision of the play that is not only cohesive in concept, but executed cohesively for the audience as well. As much as it is a small part of the process, the actor *does indeed* have to learn her or his lines; as much as it is not the most exciting aspect of the job, the director *does indeed* have to read the play over and over while conducting rehearsals. The designers, who have such an important task/burden in selecting the aesthetics of the stage and clothing and lights, *do indeed* have to do the day-to-day work like drawing renderings and hanging lights. The point being, all of these artists and craftspeople are human and have only so much time in their waking day to get the work done. A lot of the ancillary work, especially research, can fall through the cracks because there is not enough time. It is for this reason that many theatre companies and individual productions employ a **Dramaturge**.

A very brief but accurate description of a dramaturge would be this: A drama-

# 5: the dramaturge

turge is a person who helps connect all of the creative dots in a production of a play. She or he is an all-purpose assistant and problem solver.

That would be the brief description. The job of dramaturge is very wide ranging. She or he might be responsible for historical research (which in period plays can make an enormous difference) as well as researching the literary history of the play, such as finding the sources the playwright might have used in creating the story. The dramaturge often is looked at as a resource for the actors to approach when they want information such as previous interpretations and critical analyses of the play from an actor's perspective. The actors may ask for research materials that not only explain the fashion of the times, but how those fashions influenced styles of movement or expression. This is helpful knowledge that can be used to develop their characters.* All of this information can contribute immensely to the success of a show from the actor's perspective, but collecting that information is not necessarily a productive (or often even a physically possible)use of the director's time. The director might ask the dramaturge to collect materials such as paintings or songs or literary tools (critical writings, etc.) to help create a rehearsal environment that enhances the development of "the world of the play" within the cast. With regard to the literary interpretation of a script, the director quite often will ask a dramaturge to collect, read, and summarize scholarly analyses of the text. The producer

may ask the dramaturge to help with or completely conduct the securing of rights to songs or images the production plans to use, and might even be the point person who secured the rights to the play itself.

These are merely a sampling of what a dramaturge might be asked to do during a specific production. If a theatre company maintains a dramaturge for its entire season, that person may be responsible for developing new plays, and soliciting, reading, and evaluating new works. Within the construct of a theatre company, the dramaturge often has an important say in the choice of plays that go into production in the upcoming season or seasons. Ultimately, a dramaturge can be essential in defining and creating the artistic mission of the theatre company.

Credit for the term dramaturge and for the creation of the position in the world of theatre goes to the 18th-century dramatist, critic, and philosopher, Gotthold Lessing. Lessing, who was German, was a dedicated artist and lover of the theatre. He is considered one of the great minds of the Western historical period generally referred to as **The Enlightenment**. Lessing's strongest beliefs about the theatre centered on his desire to return dramatic structure to the ideals of Aristotle and his *Poetics*,

and he was a champion of the writings of Shakespeare, who, some hundred years after his death, had become somewhat unfashionable. Lessing stressed the need to look at a play within its literary and historical contexts, to explore the text beyond the bare meaning of the words. Although his desire to create a unified national theatre based in Hamburg was ultimately unsuccessful, his word, "dramaturge," and the career that it describes live on to this day.

# Suspension of Disbelief/Commitment to Character

*Tim Joyce*

One of theatre's most intriguing aspects is that it makes demands on those who consume it as well as those who create it. This is because, as an art, theatre needs to create direct communication between an audience and the performers in order to really reach its potential. The audience has to bring something to the play, and that something is known as **Suspension of Disbelief**. The theatre company, and very specifically the actors, must bring something as well, and that is called **Commitment**. Neither side in this equation can be passive if the show is truly going to succeed. As audience or as artists, we all truly must play our part. Otherwise, it simply does not work.

It is best to look at it as a contract: If the audience agrees to suspend their disbelief; the actors promise to give their full commitment to the performance.

So let's look at the terms.

Suspension of disbelief is the willingness of the audience to accept the action onstage as real. To deconstruct this is pretty simple, if you think about it. What, as an audience member, are you actually witnessing when you see a play, what is the actual phenomenon? You are in a theatre or a space that is designated as a theatre, such as a park or a public square or a warehouse. You come into this space and take a seat. At a preappointed time, the lights go down or the beginning of the play is otherwise signaled to you. Actors enter the stage area and begin to speak words that were written for them to each other. They are wearing clothes that have been picked out by a costumer, usually not their own clothes. They are more often than not bathed in artificial light and wearing makeup on their faces that is a lot thicker than the makeup people wear in public. More often than not, they are standing in front of scenery that depicts a room or a location that is not actually there. Often they are sitting in chairs or otherwise using furniture and items that were built specifically for the play and are not otherwise functional in the real world. They might even shoot one another with fake guns or stab each other with facsimiles of knives. These actors talk to each other and pretend to be other people. They pretend that their words are being thought of in that exact moment (even though they've memorized every word they are saying) and they pretend to hear and emotionally react to the words spoken to them for the first time ever each performance (even though they know, by opening night, exactly what the other actors are going to say to them). These actors pretend to live lives and events that are not actually happening but being presented as real. Ultimately, they finish the play, and usually they come out right afterward and take a bow to acknowledge the audience and thank them for being a part of the play that night.

In short, the entire play is fake. Romeo didn't actually die; an actor pretending to be Romeo pretended to die. If you want, you can wait by the stage door and tell the person who created that unreal death how moved you were by the moment in the play where they pretended to die.

The audience must suspend their disbelief. They must be willing to let go and allow themselves to experience the play as an actual series of events. There are exceptions to this, of course; some plays and productions are entirely experimental and abstract and never acknowledge the play as something to be perceived as "truth." Playwrights such as Samuel Beckett and especially Bertolt Brecht relied on breaking through and away from suspending the audience's disbelief. There are also many plays in which characters directly address the audience such as *The Laramie Project* and *The Exonerated*. Later in the book, we will talk about those kinds of theatre. However, in the majority of plays that most audience members will see in their lifetime, they are asked to accept the action onstage as real. In the vernacular, "The people in the seats have to go with it." This is the audience's half of the contract.

Suspension of disbelief is not, by the way, something that only is experienced in a play or at a movie or in front of a television. The fact is that all of us were predisposed to this concept from the moment we were children. If you watch a bunch of kids playing at a family party or a playground, you will be struck by it immediately. Children love to pretend and commit all out to it without any problem. To a small child, a spoon can be a magic wand, a table can be a spaceship. It is only as we get older that we "grow up" and stop letting our imagination overrule our skepticism.

As adults, both as audience members and actors, we have to fight that adult skepticism and reach back to our (in the best sense of the term) "childish" selves. Arguably, this is why it is called a "play" and the people performing it are called "players."

So what is the actor's part of the contract? What must exist for the performance of a play to thrive as a piece of living art? The best word for what the actors must give to the audience is commitment. (In truth, the entire production team, from the writer to the director all the way down to whoever sweeps and mops the floor of the stage must give the audience their commitment for the play to thrive. It is simply easier at this point to speak about commitment as it pertains to the actors because on the day of performance they are the most direct point of contact with the audience.) There are several layers of what this word—commitment—means to an actor. The first layer of commitment has to do with preparation. The actor owes the audience her or his work. The actors, by inviting the audience, have said that they have done the work required to make the play worthy of spending an evening and some money to experience. This includes rehearsal and learning lines and blocking, of course, but it also includes studying the craft of acting as well. To be the best artist possible, an actor must commit to developing his or her voice, movement, and interpretive skills. The actors must do whatever research may be necessary to effectively portray their roles. They must commit to being the best performers they can be at that point of their life as an artist.

However, that is only one part of commitment as it pertains to theatre artists. On the afternoon or evening of the performance, commitment comes full circle. The entire cast and crew, on the day of the show, must work together like a well-oiled machine to bring the audience and characters onstage together. The stagehands, costumers, house manager, box office reps, ushers, stage manager, and assistant stage manager(s) must concentrate and do their work. Their preparation and execution is essential to the experience. The actors must now bring it; they must commit to being as believable and vulnerable and entertaining as they can every day and every performance. They must bring their preparation to culmination in the event that is the play. The actors must bring their willingness to tap into that childish self who accepts, without embarrassment or out-of-character commentary, that they are the individual role and the person that role represents for the duration of the performance.

They have to be their character while the audience watches and allows their imagination to flow along with the play.

It is that simple. It is that complex.

If the members of the theatre production bring their commitment and the audience allows their minds to accept that the story is really happening *right then and right now*, then the art, the "magic" of theatre, if you will, occurs. We, the audience, and we, the theatre artists, have fulfilled the contract.

# mary jane masiulionis/theatre as literature/the role of the dramaturge

In order to fully describe and explain the importance and complexity of the job of Dramaturge, we spoke with Mary Jane Masiulionis, who not only has dramaturged multiple productions, but teaches theatre and its literary components at Buffalo State College. Here is what she shared with the authors.

*AS A TEACHER OF THEATRE AS BOTH LITERATURE AND A PERFORMANCE ART, WHERE DO YOU FIND COMMONALITY, AND WHERE DO YOU FIND CONTRAST?*

The commonalities are huge. Both the literary and theatrical approach to looking at a play revolve around the love of the author's world; the historical and theoretical influences that led that writer to create that work. It is relevant for both literary readers and theatre artists to understand that history and art intertwine; there have been many different historical artistic periods and movements. The evolution of expression and how theatre and the arts and poetry were brought together in meetings of artists throughout history is important for anyone to explore. The political and aesthetic arguments that occurred in the Fin de Siècle Salons of Paris (circa 1880 to 1900 approximately) or the banter and competition found in the spirit of the Algonquin Round Table and its cadre of writers and artists all have shaped the modern theatre. These analytical arguments continue today and they demonstrate that theatre isn't this unreachable esoteric entity in space; but rather a living literary and creative art that is neither irrelevant nor distant from our daily lives. As for the differences, well, academically speaking Literary Analysis focuses on the meaning of the words as written and read. Theatre is of course also dependent upon analysis but that analysis is focused more upon the action of the words and how to transport the text onto the stage as a live event.

*WHAT SHOULD AN INTRO TO THEATRE STUDENT KNOW BY THE END OF SEMESTER?*

They should know the importance of community [in the theatre]. Theatre is not just one person; it is a live, in-the-moment event, which is transferred into an immediate moment. Theatre is a chance to create an art in concert with other people that changes and grows. Oh and yes, they should also know this:

"It's not just about men in tights."

† he practicalities of designing and building the costumes for a play call for a variety of working skills as well as theoretical and historical knowledge. The production of any play is powerfully enhanced when the costuming is effective, and the limits of what a Costumer gets to do on any particular project more often have less to do with creative inspiration and more to do with limitations of budget and available manpower. To get an insight into the challenges and rewards of getting costumes on the characters in a play designed and built by opening night, the author spoke to Ann Emo, an accomplished costume professional who teaches the craft to aspiring professionals in a college setting. These are the insights she generously shared with us.

# 6: the costume designer

# costuming as craft, ann emo interview

*HOW DID YOU PERSONALLY BECOME A COSTUME PROFESSIONAL, WHERE WERE YOU TRAINED IN THE CRAFT?*

I received a Masters in Costume Design from NYU and from there went on to work with the Santa Fe Opera, The McCarter Theatre in Princeton, New Jersey; The Long Wharf Theatre of New Haven Connecticut, after which I began working for the largest and most important costume shop in New York City, Barbara Matera Ltd. The time I spent with Matera was a very exciting time for Broadway Theatre and I got to work on costumes for shows like "LaCage Aux Folles" and "Nine." I was doing the hard work that a shop like that demands such as building, stitching, and cutting material for costumes and costume pieces. This was good experience and I made very good connections in the business while I was there although my Masters work at NYU was based on my desire to be a Designer rather than a technician. The practical experience was very helpful however.

*YOU USED SOME TERMS JUST NOW THAT ARE PART AND PARCEL TO YOUR CAREER, DO YOU MIND DEFINING SOME OF THEM FOR THE AVERAGE THEATRE-GOER?*

Sure. First of all there is the Designer. This is the person who conceives the look and appropriateness of the costumes for the production. They do the overall concept that the technicians then execute to create the actual costume pieces. In theatrical costuming a Technician refers to a variety of different skills and crafts. You have Beaders, who do the beading and embroidery the costumes might require. There are Crafters, whose task is to create specialty pieces. Milliners; technicians who specialize in the building of hats. Special Effects creators who are responsible for making costume pieces such as blood bags, breakaway clothing such as the breakaway dress used in the Broadway production of "Sunday In The Park With George." They may also may be asked to create elements that include specialty dying of material, and the painting and crafting of masks and puppetry such as you see in shows like "The Lion King." [Where the Director Julie Taymor collaborated with Michael Curry (One of the most highly respected Puppetry Artists in the American Theatre) to create complex and beautiful pieces that needed to also allow the actors wearing them to move in dynamic ways.] In a costume shop you will also find technicians who specialize in Shoes, Costume Props like fans purses and jewelry, and it is important to mention that Hair and Make Up are essential areas related to and often intertwined with costume work. The Costume Tech people face other challenges like creating costumes that allow actors to dance or do stage Combat which might include working with swords, knives, or whatever weapons the Director calls for. There's a lot of work available in a Costume Shop.

*YOU USED A TERM THAT RESONATES THROUGHOUT THIS ENTIRE BOOK, A TERM THAT IS INTRINSIC TO THE THINKING OF THEATRICAL PROFESSIONALS, THAT WE'D LOVE TO KNOW YOUR DEFINITION OF. THAT WORD IS "COLLABORATION." WHAT DOES COLLABORATION IN THEATRE MEAN TO YOU PERSONALLY?*

My design philosophy is this: I am there to support the execution of a production, to create the environment the story is portraying and to help the performers become who they are. I need to set time period and work within the stage space. Once you've gone past the world premiere of a play, most playwrights allow the new artists to hone the piece in subsequent or ongoing productions. I recently designed the costumes for a production of "A Delicate Balance" at the Irish Classical Theatre Company. The audience needs to know that in the world of the play the year is 1968. Edward Albee, the play's author, was very particular about his demands for set design and look. He was **not** open to allowing new artists to reinterpret his pieces very far from what his script called for. Because clothing styles change more often, as opposed to the slower pace of change in furniture and home decoration, costume was in this case an easier way to denote the specific period; especially given that this play portrays fairly conservative people in conflict with characters who are non-comformists. The clothes can set period faster than the set can. "A Delicate Balance" takes place in a country estate. The stage design therefore may not portray specific historical context as quickly or accurately as costumes can.

Another function of the costume [within the context of Collaboration] is to help the actor get past their persona and find their character. The best thing that can happen to me in a fitting is for an actor to put on a costume piece and say "Aha! Now I know who I am." This is especially gratifying in costuming a contemporary play. I want to give the actors a tool to facilitate being a different person when they are onstage. I need to know the text and have an understanding of the psychology of the character and the actor playing that character. If I'm doing my job effectively my costumes help the actors define the differences between themselves and their characters. Costumes have to have a cohesive look. It is a multilayered task; being visually interesting while working with the character/actor needs. Costume design doesn't stop at the clothing; it is the whole look of the performer, wigs, makeup, accoutrements, jewelry, and hairstyles.

## WHAT TOOLBOX SKILLS DOES A COSTUME DESIGNER NEED TO WORK IN THE BUSINESS?

Amazingly, they actually do not need to know how to sew! They need to be able to communicate their designs to the stitchers and cutters. Now that isn't to say that technical stitching, cutting, and patterning skills are not highly valuable to have but honestly they are not absolutely required. A Costume designer must have a good working knowledge of Fashion History and Period Styles. You must be a good interpretive reader with the ability to comprehend and analyze a script. I cannot design effective costumes if I am not skilled in the art of character analysis. And then there are the technical requirements of the script. Does a specific character need a wet raincoat because the dialog in the play has a line that refers to that character wearing one? A lot of the costume requirements of characters can come from what other characters might say about what they were wearing or how they look [ed.] Quick changes need to be determined in the script analysis; contemporary play scripts tend to create challenges this way because a lot of playwrights think visually like film/tv people. In live theatre this is a problem because we *don't have the ability to stop the action and change someone's clothes, then re-start.* Communication skills are vital, both visual and verbal. You cannot do a costume fitting with just pictures and you can't communicate to a shop or director with only words. A Costume Designer needs to have a full understanding of design elements; shape, color, mass … Again here comes that term again: A Costume Designer must be able to collaborate.

It's not as easy as it looks. It is not just about picking clothes out of a closet. The job is to create a cohesive environment in which the characters in the play can exist.

Students should absolutely understand this about theatre, regardless of whether they are taking the class to fulfill an Art requirement or exploring the possibility of becoming involved in theatre themselves: In theatre, when a production is being created of a play, ***NO CHOICE SHOULD BE ARBITRARY.*** In the theatre Collaboration should never be just a buzzword, it should be an applied reality. I say this, in true Collaboration 1+1 = 5. And by that I mean that the sum quality of the work can exceed the number of people working on the project if they work together and respect everyone's ideas and talent.

And the theatre majors should really know this: ***Technical theatre work; the Backstage, Preproduction, Design, Building, Run Crew people and all of the so called "behind the scenes" tasks they perform are essential.*** TECHNICAL STUFF GETS YOU THE MOST EMPLOYMENT.

*OKAY, WE'VE TALKED A LOT ABOUT THE CHALLENGES AND HARD WORK, BUT AS A COSTUMER DESIGNER, WHAT WOULD YOU SAY IS THE FUN PART?*

Oh that's easy, collaborating with fun, talented, and creative people. Within the actual work the fun part is identifying and solving what you and the Director see as the biggest challenges. I think about the character of Feste in Shakespeare's Twelfth Night. Most Directors of Shakespeare plays will tell you that Feste is the most enigmatic character in the play, so, how do you get the character who is most enigmatic in a text to work? How do you explain for both the audience and the actor, through costume among all the other design elements, who this character really is?[1] Or think about Shakespeare's Richard III, you can see the same challenge there as well. Richard himself, very early in the play, describes himself as being physically repulsive to the point of hideousness. However, within minutes of his very denigrating characterization of his appearance, he seduces Princess Anne in the presence of her father's corpse [a corpse by the way that is dead because Richard himself killed him, a few months after Richard stabbed Anne's husband to death; a pretty good job of seducing given the circumstances...] So given his description of that odious appearance combined with his seductive power, how does a Costume Designer facilitate these completely divergent and contradictory aspects of the character? You've got to come to consensus with the Actor and the Director about challenges like this. You've got to work in synch

---

1    Feste is a Jester; but he also functions as a commentator and conscience to the main characters in "Twelfth Night." This counterintuitive character trait manifests especially in two seemingly romantic but enigmatically sad songs he sings; "Oh Mistress Mine" and "The Rain It Raineth Every Day." These songs and Feste's wisdom, hidden in seemingly absurd quotes that upon a second hearing are truly profound, make this one of Shakespeare's more enigmatic characters and therefore a challenge to costume as well as act. In this manner Feste shares a lot with The Fool in "King Lear" as well.

with all of the people involved; you aren't in a void. Again I love the challenges the script gives to me, and I love solving them as best I can in collaboration with everyone involved.

*AND WHAT ARE THE OBSTACLES YOU FACE?*

One of the most challenging things about costume design is the "people factor." You may design a perfect rendering, but when you get the actual human being playing the role in the shop, elements of the original design might not work and you have to be able to work with who the artist actually is both physically and creatively. Sometimes you get 6 months and can build the look from scratch, sometimes you are finding premade costumes and adapting them.

You have to know where you are going to get the pieces and either find or build them. In lower budget theatre you are doing a lot of accommodating, your budget might not have the space for 20 suits that might cost $200 each. You are dependent on your resources.

You must have research skills to find sources and visuals for pieces. Current events, politics, religion, you have to know about these things because theatre is a slice of life. Although everybody knows how to put clothes on not everyone knows how to make the right choice.

The best of possible worlds: You get your play, read it, research it, talk about the challenges you have found with the entire creative team at the first design meeting and develop your designs from the start with the director's concepts at the core. I can say "this is the [time] period" so if the characters wear high heels, the Set Designer can take that into account when designing stairs and other set elements that are affected by the shoes of the period and their movement limitations. Successful Designers [Costume, Light, Set, Sound, Etc.] do not work parallel; they work best enmeshed.

# erica fire, costuming interview

We know that the costume designer is responsible for the renderings and the overall concept of costuming a play. But if the clothes cannot be found or purchased, which happens frequently, they need to be built. That's why there are costume shops, and in the world of theatre they employ a lot of people. We talked to Erica Fire, a veteran of many professional costume shops, to explain who is there, and how the work gets done.

*WHAT IS YOUR TRAINING/EXPERTISE? WHEN DID IT BECOME A CAREER OPTION IN YOUR MIND?*

I wanted to work in costuming really since high school and so I went to college with the idea for learning costume design. But in college, I became more interested in the technical aspects of building a costume; figuring out what the flat pattern pieces are and how to turn them into a 3 dimensional piece that an actor can wear. I got my BA at Bennington; but I really got the bulk of my useful knowledge at the "school of hard knocks." First I worked at a fabric store, then I got a summer job with Santa Fe Opera. While there I worked on the same draping team with a woman at Studio Arena, a LORT [Professional Equity Not For Profit] Theatre in Buffalo . Then I worked at GeVa [also LORT] in Rochester New York. It is at GeVa where I learned tailoring.

Define a costume shop, who'd be there?

A costume shop is the workshop where the costumes are built, fitted, and altered. It is the place where the physical work of costumes gets done. Often it is a separate company that takes bids from theatres as opposed to being a part of an individual theatrical company. New York City has many independent shops which entertain bids from shows. There are shops of all sizes, some very large, some very small, and there are of course many costume shops based in colleges with Theatre departments. Let's look at how the big shops work.

Jobs in a big shop, shops that build costumes for major Shakespeare festivals, opera companies, and the larger LORT companies, would include:

Costume Director: This person is in charge of the big picture. Responsible for the budget and staying within it, personnel, what gets built in the shop or outside, and she/he decides what needs to be rented (as opposed to built) for a particular production. Usually this person finds themself working far ahead of opening night and works directly with the designer and production manager. The costume director often decides the costume budget breakdown of a particular show or a season. They are in charge of wardrobe, the main shop, and the craft shop. [Costume crafts includes hats, shoes, armor, jewelry, SFX[2] like blood bags, paint effects,

---

2   "SFX" is the short term used in the entertainment industry when referring to Special Effects.

*Make-up is considered part of Costume Design*

lights on costume, dying or distressing of fabric] They make the decisions and deals regarding any outside jobbing like boots, hats, or specialty items.

Office Assistant: This person is the business organizer and handles the paperwork and budget logistics.

Shopper: This person acquires materials: from big orders such as fabric, to small day to day details such as new sewing machine needles/parts and unanticipated building contingencies.

Floor Manager: This is the person in a shop who manages supplies and individual workloads. He or she assigns work to individual draping teams (Draping teams work with dress forms, cutting tables, etc.) The floor manager often schedules fittings, all the while making sure that construction of costumes runs on time. The floor manager has to work well with costume director. It's vitally important that there is cohesion between them.

Draping Teams: These folks are either called a draper, the cutter/draper, or the tailor, although the term "tailor" applies to menswear only. Some shops divide teams by men or women. Specializing in tailoring makes a costume builder more valuable since most men's suits are purchased and tailored, while most women's are built from scratch.

Draper or Pattern Maker: This person drapes cut cloth on a dress form or drafts with rulers to create the patterns for the cutters to make the fabric pieces for building. They do fittings, and adjusting of the pattern. Most costumes start with a mock up version, often made of muslin or stretch material. This mockup is used to adjust the pattern before cutting the more expensive fabric.

Stitchers: They are also called sewers, but most prefer stitchers because they do not want the sanitary implication the word has when you read it on a page. They do the actual sewing.

What skill set does a costume tech need to work and compete in the industry? You must be able to sew by hand, machine, and industrial machine, quickly and accurately. You have to have good math and comprehension skills, to recognize quick changes and character needs. A costume tech needs to possess Geometry and other applicable math conception skills. Good interpersonal skills are a must to work under deadline with a team under stress. You have to have motor skill with your hands. There is an unteachable "touch" to it; an ability to handle fabric that cannot necessarily be taught and many years of sewing experience is needed to get good at it. Costume techs need to think spacially to mentally get from a 2 dimensional rendering to 3 dimensional realities. Most pieces are sewn inside out; so you have to be able to envision how a piece inverts as you sew it. Otherwise you can end up creating an unusable unwearable costume piece. No one wants to end up making a "Moebius vest" for an actor.

In short, the designer is the artist; and the tech is the engineer.

Carol Beckley is a well-respected and highly experienced professional Set Designer working out of Western New York. She is also a stage technician, and she teaches both of those aspects to college students at Buffalo State. Many of the students she teaches are themselves aspiring artists and designers. In order to understand the task of being a Set Designer the Author sat down with her and asked her some questions about the craft and the business of Set Design. We wanted to get a look at the mindset of a professional in this area. We wanted to hear both the artistic challenges as well as the practicalities. As always it is important to include this caveat: what she expresses here fits into the overview of how set design works in general, but you will, most likely, be able to find people in the field who might disagree with some of her viewpoints. This is of course because, as in all of the jobs that people do in theatre, designing a set is an art as well as a craft. The beauty of theatre is that the how and why will always be open for debate because right and wrong aren't the point. The point will always be realizing the production: telling the story the play has to tell within the unavoidable confines of time, money, and the desires of the entire creative team. Here's what Carol had to say about the Set Design aspect of

# 7: the set designer

the theatre, including both its challenges and rewards, as she personally has experienced it in her professional career.

# carol beckley, set design interview

*WHEN DID SET DESIGN BECOME A CAREER OPTION IN YOUR MIND?*

I went through five different Undergraduate Majors. In my second year of Grad School I fully committed to the realization that my life was going to be in the theatre.

*AS BOTH A TEACHER OF THE CRAFT AND AN ACTIVE SET DESIGNER, WHAT INFORMATION DO YOU THINK AN "INTRO TO THEATRE" TEXTBOOK ABSOLUTELY MUST CONTAIN ABOUT THIS CAREER PATH?*

I would hope that after taking an Intro class that the students would be able to think like a set designer. I'd hope they left the class with an idea of what the term means and how it is done. I'd like the students who finish an Intro course to understand the kinds of things a set designer thinks about and how they make visual choices.

*SO IN YOUR EXPERIENCE, HOW IS IT DONE?*

Three to six months before opening night, the set designers begin their process (developing the design.) This is done in collaboration with the director. The designers work with her or his concept to visually support the Director's interpretation of the text. Conceptual work in my opinion should be done, on any individual play, during the first one or two months of the process. Through a series of meetings with the director the entire creative team designs the visual world of the play. Ideally, Set, Light and Costume are done concurrently, but elements like time and budget do not always leave this as a possibility. It is important that all visual elements and storytelling aspects are in sync with the director developing the world that the play will exist in. The ideas are bounced back and forth among the entire creative team, and generally this all happens in a series of meetings discussing the world of the play (both the director's vision along with the playwright's intent)with everyone sharing visual research, imagery, ideas, and sketches. We are selecting the imagery that resonates with the director's vision.

*PLEASE EXPLAIN MODEL CONSTRUCTION:*

A Model Box is used. 3D MODELING; Anyway the designer can best communicate the environment. Ultimately the result of the meetings is getting the director's vision done, getting the director to say "You took my adjectives and turned them into a visual reality." You do not work before meeting with the director; you read the play and then find out his intention.

2009 Buffalo State production of The Grapes of Wrath

*WHAT SKILL SETS DO YOU FIND ESSENTIAL IN A SET DESIGNER?*

First of all Creativity. It is also important to know how to conduct scholarly inquiry into history and historical periods, and understand the "why" of the characters within their historical period (I.E. Vietnam, the Elizabethan Era, Ancient Greece.) A good Set Designer needs to be able to read and interpret a text, be a detective, find the words in the play that inform the scenery. Of course the ability to draw (either mechanical drawing, drafting, or computer modeling) is something a Set Designer needs to have a handle on. I need to have the ability to think visually, and then I need to know how to communicate the visual concept I have for the set to the director and audience. And then there are of course the Toolbox Skills.

*2012 Buffalo State production of* Fuddy Mears

*PLEASE TELL US, WHAT ARE THOSE "TOOLBOX SKILLS?"*

Well I'm talking about skills like drafting and Mechanical Perspective Drawing. Designers need to have an understanding of construction techniques (i.e. how a flat is made) and what is actually possible. A knowledge of Art History, which includes sculpture, upholstery, and period styles, is essential. You'd better know carpentry because you can't draft it if you don't know how to build it. A knowledge of materials like lumber, metals, fabrics, soft goods, foams, polymers, paints and finishes. An understanding of mechanics of the space, [meaning the individual theatre space in which a show is being produced] understand its sight lines and the relationship of the stage to its audience. A Set Designer must be able to adapt to each and every space she works in and have an understanding of that theatre company's audience in order to create a set that resonates with the prospective or targeted audience's age and demographics. You need an understanding of architecture and construction methods through history. [A Set Designer needs] a strong awareness of the visual styles and styles of architecture throughout history. What you *do not* need to know is how a Victorian craftsman created a Cornice. You need to know what that Cornice looks like and understand its scale and the finish of it. Then you need to know how to replicate that Cornice using modern scenic materials which could be anything from lumber to foam to vacufoam. And the Set Designer needs to do this all within budget.

A set has a different perspective than real life. Even on a film location you are sculpting through a camera's perspective. My primary goal is to get the audience to believe the set is true to the spirit of whatever period style I'm portraying, even if I have to be inaccurate to do it. Using costume as an example, you see that beautiful Renaissance Gown an actress might be wearing? It might have a zipper because that actress needs to do a quick change. Method does not take precedence over telling the story. If your goal is to teach the actual period style, as in a History Channel documentary, then yes, the purity of it is important, but historical accuracy doesn't take precedence over the story or its message. My set is there to serve the play.

*2010 Buffalo State production* Seven Keys to Baldpate

*WHAT WOULD YOU SAY, ESSENTIALLY, IS THE SET DESIGNER'S TASK?*

All of the designers, as well as the playwright, director, and actors, are there to set the mood and bring forth an emotional response from the audience. As Set Designers we can alter the audience's response to that character, good, bad or indifferent, even before they hear them come on stage and talk. Scenery can strongly influence individual reactions to the people on stage. This is also true of costumes, lights, makeup, and sound. It is the Set Designers job to get the audience into a visual mindset that prepares them for the world of the play, from the moment you enter and see the set. There is a great amount of work that goes into research. For instance you can look for eight hours for an essential prop and not find it. If you can't ultimately find it, you have to build it. Designing sets exclusively for plays is not necessarily a viable career choice; if you are going to do theatre exclusively you will probably need to augment your income through other uses of your skills, like teaching, or designing and building sets for film, television, and commercials. You do not have enough time to do enough stage plays in a year solely to make a living because each theatre project is a time consuming process. Designing the set for a play takes months if you are going to do it right.

† heatrical lighting is both scientific and mystical. There are many occasions in theatre where a low-budget production of a play has to make choices about elements of technical design based solely on money. The production might not be able to afford elaborate sets or effects or costumes. Lighting in theatre becomes magic in these instances. A lighting designer, with a minimum of equipment, can create a stage where day becomes night, a living room becomes a forest, or fire consumes a building. Light can be manipulated, plotted, and focused wherever the director and designer want. The mood of a scene, whether warm, sad, erotic, or homicidal, can be effectively conferred simply through the use of colored gels in front of high-powered lamps. At the high end of the scale, with a large budget and the freedom of time, the number of effects the **Lighting Designer** can create becomes breathtaking. Dracula can swoop in from the rafters on wires while the light on stage splashes from an eerie electric blue to a shocking blood red. Collaboration once again becomes key, in the sense that all of this needs to be worked into the play within the concept of the director and the message of the playwright. The lighting designer, set designer, costume designer, and sound designer, when they work

# 8: the lighting designer

in confluence with a director with a vision and actors who are fearless, can all come together to make art that is not only entertaining but world changing. This may seem hyperbolic, saying that a person with a grid of lights and a set of dimmers can create eras of time, location, and emotion, but it is not. All over the world in theatres, lighting designers make this happen every day.

In an attempt to better understand the process of lighting design, we interviewed Shannon Schweitzer, a career lighting designer who also teaches the craft to emerging professionals. He had some very insightful things to tell us.

# shannon schweitzer, lighting interview

*AS A LIGHTING DESIGNER ASSIGNED TO A SPECIFIC PRODUCTION, WHAT IS THE PREP WORK INVOLVED?*

Long before opening night is when the prep work begins. To do my job well I need to read the script several times, analyzing it as a story and knowing it well enough to anticipate the needs of the play when it comes time to light it. I not only need to pick out specifics such as the time, place, and the overall emotional tone of the play, there are practicalities to consider, such as whether the rooms are lit by windows, or whether the play even takes place indoors. Are there references to good or bad weather? What is the totality of the environment? For instance, if the play has a scene where two characters watch a sunset, well, where are they watching it? What time of year is it? Sunset in Buffalo during late January is very different than a sunset in June in Hawaii.

I need to confer with the director to get her/his ideas about the play. How does the Director want to tell the story? Is the look going to be very realistic or will it be an abstract environment like a painting by Dali? I do a lot of research into the time period, and the tastes of the time. In my personal approach to research, I get a lot from looking at paintings, and considering the angles of my light design needs given the space the play takes place in. Going back to the sunset example, there are aesthetic questions that I have to ask such as "What does a sunset look like in real life?" To make that light, the sunset light, how do I use my instruments and implement it into my design? Or going back to the question of windows, if the room is illuminated by window light, what is effective in creating that tone and mood?

Once the process has moved forward I like to go to rehearsals. I go to a lot of them and start writing where specific cues may be in the script as the show is evolving. All the while there is constant emailing between the director and the entire design team. The work doesn't begin and end at the theatre or in my office, a lot of times I wake up at 4 a.m. with a solution to a problem that has been bugging me for weeks.

*2007 Buffalo State production of* Antigone

Eventually rehearsal and all the communication reaches the point where it is time for me to do the paperwork. The paperwork includes creating the cue sheet, creating renderings of the light plot, and mapping the channel hookup. Six months after the initial production meetings I'm finally in the actual space hanging and focusing the lights and cuing the show. Then it is time for **Tech Rehearsal**, where the cues are set in conference with the director and the director's needs. The director will look at each light cue, with sets and costumes and actors, and then comment

*2013 Buffalo State original production of* When the Walls Come Tumbling Down

upon whether my levels and colors are working in his or her opinion. If not, then I adjust the specifics to fit what the director desires.

*HOW DID YOU DEVELOP THIS APPROACH TO YOUR WORK?*

My personal approach to lighting design evolved through an awful lot of trial and error. I've had a lot of mentors, or should I say people I've worked for and with who've used techniques that I discovered also worked for me. Other methods [used by other lighting designers] aren't wrong, they don't work for me. For my work to be good, it has to be "my method." I want to use what works best for me and gets the work done efficiently and with good aesthetics. In the final analysis, on any production of a play, I'm just another paintbrush trying to give the director his/her painting. Most members of the design team seem to feel this way, not just the lighting people. And when it comes to that collaboration between the designers and reaching the same vision you have to be able to give and take. It can get tense but you pull it together. And of course, there are the inevitable restrictions of money and time. I studied lighting as an undergrad and in graduate school at Michigan State, but the best education I got in learning to do this work was doing hands-on work in New York City, being led by people who are at the top of their profession. When the guy standing next to you helping you choose a gel for a light is a guy who *actually has a gel named for him* you realize quickly this is someone to watch and learn from.

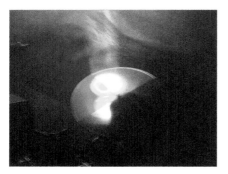
*Motorized Colored Gel*

First, it is essential that you are comfortable working with various personalities. This may seem funny, but in my experience younger lighting designers are more likely to say no, or resist the director when they ask for a change in a cue or an effect. That to me seems counterintuitive. You would think a lighting designer with 20 years of Broadway experience would be more protective of his or her work, but that's usually not the case. I think this is because older, more experienced designers are more experienced with collaboration; they know being asked to change something in their design isn't personal, it is about creating the best work possible. A lighting designer needs to have basic electrical knowledge, but they don't have to know all of the theory that a union electrician might know because lighting for the stage is totally different than doing it in your house. You do need practical knowledge such as how dimmers work, or how many lights can go on one circuit without shorting it out. I, and for that matter any lighting person, need to know basic math, and I do mean basic things like how to add and subtract. Unfortunately not everyone knows that kind of basic stuff. Lighting designers need a good grounding knowledge of science and have a mastery of photometrics. The primary colors of light are **Red, Green, and Blue**, and there are 6.5 million color combos you can make using those three colors of light. Combining colored light is different than combining pigment. In lighting, green and magenta makes white, which is not true if you combine green and magenta crayons. Light is thought of in terms of cool and warm colors. I have to be able to color coordinate, know how gels work with different textures; light reflecting off of wood or plastic looks very different than light reflecting off of fabric. It all falls under the heading of **Lighting Color Theory**.

What I want students who read this book or take my Intro to Theatre class to know when the semester ends is this: I basically want them to have learned how to interpret their vision with light on their own stage. It isn't important to me that they leave with a thorough knowledge of Ohm's Law. What I'd like them to know is how to go into their own bedroom and set up the lighting to create any mood or environment they want. 

,

Creating a production of a play requires work both on a small and a large scale, from small details like hanging a sconce on a wall to overall coordination of the various technical aspects. The person charged with the job of complete oversight of all the elements of production is known as the **Production Manager**. She or he is responsible for coordinating the construction and loading of scenery, production and care of costuming, as well as implementing the lighting, sound, and all inclusive technical aspects of any theatrical presentation. Usually the production manager is the highest-ranking person, the "go-to" authority on the production staff of a theatre company or a theatrical house. Included among the duties of a typical production manager are many logistics, including procurement of rehearsal and performance space for the play. In order to get a hands-on insight into the day-to-day work this job entails, we spoke to John Malinowski. John is the production manager of the Burchfield-Penney Center and as such oversees not only productions of plays but all manner of presentations, including art installations, music, and educational conferences. This is what he had to share with us.

# 9: the production manager and technical director

# john malinowski, production interview

*CAN YOU TELL US WHAT WAS YOUR TRAINING, THE BACKGROUND THAT LED YOU TO THIS POSITION?*

After undergraduate studies I decided to go to grad school. So I went to URTA.[1] Out of 18 schools that I interviewed with I ended up touring three. I chose the University of Illinois and studied in their "Scenic Technology" program. From there I was hired as the Assistant Technical Director for the Studio Arena Theatre in Buffalo. It was a great time to be working there. I gained a great deal of knowledge about how theatre works in the professional world as opposed to theatre in the academic world. Among the obvious technical and building skills, there was something essential that I hadn't ever been taught about that I learned at the Studio Arena. I learned to network. All over the country, whether it is in Austin, Texas, Seattle, Washington, or New York City, I found that the theatrical world consisted of a very tight community everywhere in theatre. To work consistently, to make a living, a stage technician has got to know the people who both work in and do the hiring in the industry. While I loved working at the Studio Arena, unfortunately it went out of business. I worked the last season there. When it closed, because of my technical and networking skills I was able to continue working 70–80 hours a week.

*SO WHAT WOULD BE YOUR ADVICE TO A YOUNG PROFESSIONAL ENTERING THE THEATRE WORLD?*

I tell students this all the time: become someone who can say "yes" to projects. For two years I never said "no" to a project or a job, and that includes everything from loading trucks to working as the Assistant Technical Director of Shakespeare in Delaware Park [in Buffalo]. I learned early on that you have to have both technical and social skills to work consistently.

*DO YOU HAVE TO LIVE IN NEW YORK OR L.A. TO MAKE A LIVING IN TECH THEATRE?*

Not at all. You can make a living in a medium market in tech theatre as long as you have 3 things:

1. Skills;
2. Network in town that needs the skills;
3. A positive attitude; one that says "I'll never say 'no' to a job."

---

1  The national unified auditions and interviews held by the University/Resident Theatre Association (URTA).

I tell students to work anywhere they can because every situation has different approaches
and techniques regarding technical works. Each
theatre, each production has its own unique look
and concept. So the more you work with different
people the more you know how to work within
varying parameters of space, interpretation,
budget, etc.

*Production Manager 's studio*

### *WHAT IS ESSENTIAL, IN YOUR OPINION, TO BEING AN EFFECTIVE PRODUCTION MANAGER?*

You must have the ability to come into a new
space and work with its strengths and weaknesses. You have to adapt to the peculiarities of
any space. This is essential. The acoustics and
sightlines of each and every different venue are never the same and often completely different.
For instance I might find myself working with Shakespeare in Delaware Park during the summer
and then with Road Less Travelled Theatre in the fall. They could [not] possibly be any more
different: one is huge [a public park with seating for over 2000], and one is tiny [a Black Box
space that seats 50]. Creating set pieces for both requires different skills and knowledge. There
are many different effective ways to approach these challenges too. A wise production manager
once said to me: "Nobody gets into arguments unless two people have different ideas and both
are effective approaches. You have to decide then, whose effective methods do you work with?"
Ultimately a big part of the job is making choices and going with them.

### *WHAT WOULD YOU SAY IS THE "PRODUCTION MANAGER'S TOOLBOX?"*

As production manager I manage any events in the building. I must know how to work with
lighting, sound, and video for a 159-seat venue. The events can range from a poetry reading
with a mike and 1 light to hanging large swathes of cloth and multiple lights, sound, and video
for a major art installation. I need to be able to light and install an art piece and use my theatre
tech skills to make the artist's vision work as they desire. I have to implement training for my
people in the various theatrical protocols for all of the events that need to be covered. I have to
understand and implement the needs of clients who rent the theatre space. This has to be done
within the limits of time, budget, and technical limits. This can include issues as varied as major
technical and electrical issues to implementing work off of an artist's laptop into a PowerPoint
presentation. I want to make whomever rents the space look as good as possible in the space and
achieve their goals visually, sonically, and artistically.

I have to be on top of the latest and greatest technologies, and this includes not only technical
knowledge, but also finding the grant money to pay for the best equipment available.

*The scenery van of the Old Vic Travelling Theatre Company rumbles past pit heads whilst on tour in South Wales. The manager, Paul Smythe, can just be seen in the back of the van, which is actually an old furniture removal van.*

I'd look for knowledge of construction and carpentry, as well as a facility for basic math. A carpenter needs to be very good at fractions, but she does not have to be a genius in trig. You need to understand design capabilities of different spaces and materials. My replacement would need to be effective under the crunch of a deadline and be able to fix any unexpected problems that can and do crop up. You have to be able to create set pieces that look like they have the weight and bulk they really have, but are in fact not as heavy as they look. I'd want the candidate to have taken all of the classes required to design safe set pieces. I'd expect her to know **Rigging Safety** and proper **OSHA Safety Protocols**. The sets you build must first and foremost be safe. Therefore you must know the mathematics of safety principles such as how to calculate a platform's weight capacity. A production manager must know how to use materials safely and understand the engineering design factors behind the weight limit. Best case, you aim to build a platform that can handle 10 times the weight it will actually be holding during the show. I take this all very seriously. When I'm technical director for a show I do not allow anyone else to walk on a set piece such as a staircase until I've walked it. Until I know it is ready. I rope off all unfinished pieces for safety. I love the job, but it is very complex. It is so difficult when the set and costumes and all the other pieces of the puzzle are getting close to opening night for everyone to coordinate. You still need to have production meetings right up to opening to coordinate safety and concept. I hate to do anything twice! Measure twice, cut once. Improperly cut or designed wood and materials can hurt the budget. A tech is constantly improving techniques to ensure the best quality that you can while eliminating mistakes and saving money. I recommend *The Backstage Handbook* to any student who is planning to work backstage or in design. They really should read this. The final advice I give to students is this:

Learn to say "thank you" and "please" even under the stress of an 80-hour week. If you are nice and polite, you'll get more work compared to someone with similar skills who isn't.

The best thing about theatre is that there is nothing impossible, you just have to figure out how [to] make it happen within your space, time, budget, and manpower concerns.

,

erhaps no individual member of the production team is more vital to the actual delivery of a play from the page to the stage than the **Stage Manager**. This woman or man is charged with the task of coordinating all of the creative and technical elements of a production. Not only must she or he attend all production meetings, but every rehearsal of the play as well. Duties of the stage manager include the overall coordination of schedules, running efficient rehearsals (especially in Equity productions, where the union is quite adamant about assuring that rehearsal begins and ends exactly according to what is scheduled, making sure that changes to that schedule are not unilateral decisions by the director or producer), recording of cues, blocking, line changes, props, or any new costume or set pieces that may become necessary during rehearsal, and in cases where there is no assistant to the director, following book for the actors and recording the director's notes at individual rehearsals. ("**Following Book**" means reading along with the script as the actors speak their lines. When an actor loses a line or forgets, the actor calls out, "Line, please," and the stage manager gives it to them.) If an actor has incorrectly remembered or is paraphrasing her or his dialogue, it is the job of the stage

# 10: the stage manager

manager to point it out to them.

Incredibly, that is not all the job of stage manager entails. While doing all of this hands-on work during rehearsal, a stage manager also is one of the overseers of the construction of sets, costumes, implementation of light design, and the entire technical half of the show. Production managers and technical directors in theatre companies that can afford those positions have the final say on technical implementation and construction, but it is in no way uncommon for a stage manager to be responsible for all of those duties as well.

Often the stage manager is responsible for giving the actors notes after opening night. The freelance nature of theatre as a career means that most directors aren't available to come and keep track of the growth of the play once the run has begun. Hopefully the director has moved on to the next production they are directing. In order to assure that the play doesn't lose its shape or the concepts that the director worked on, the stage manager gives notes. This is a subtle process when you give it thought. A play grows from opening night to closing night. It is hoped this growth is a reflection of the actors deepening their connection to the cores of their characters and the similar growth in their fellow actors' work. This can go wrong, however—sometimes a performer, wittingly or not, alters what she or he is doing in ways that hurt the production.

*Hal Holbrook,* Stage Manager in Our Town

A stage manager, in this instance, has to keep the shape together and bring the work back into focus. Telling an actor that they are making mistakes or unwanted changes to the production after opening night is a situation that can cause some tension, and this is definitely a part of the art in being a stage manager. (Toward that end, it is really no surprise that stage managers belong to the same union as actors, the Actors' Equity Association.)

The stage manager also calls the cues during the show, telling the stagehands and tech crew when to implement effects in lighting, set, and sound, according to the cues that were set during tech rehearsal. The stage manager creates a **Master Book of Cues** (or perhaps a file in the computer board) that has every technical cue coordinated with its place in the play, down to the lines spoken, which spurs it. The stage manager makes sure that the actors are in place for scenes, and for that matter makes sure that the actors and entire crew are kept aware of the number of minutes left before the play begins as everyone sets up their section or puts on their makeup and costume, so there's nobody unprepared or out of place when the curtain rises.

The fact is that a stage manager must understand every single aspect of how a play is written, acted, directed, and built, and she or he has to know how to oversee the creation of the actual production of the script. Stage managers, in brief, literally get the show done. Aside from knowledge of creative/technical aspects up to and including how to use a hammer or direct an actor (without using the hammer to direct the actor), a stage manager must possess one quality or it is unlikely she or he will see career success: Organization. Without that quality, the job would overwhelm the person holding it and the production of the play itself would be in danger of falling apart. Any conversation with a person who has worked in the theatrical world will back up this assertion: a stage manager can make or break a show and is one of the most important contributors to the success of any production.

*Sound Board*

# part two: theatre–the space, **style**, and **history**

a conversation with any experienced actor or director about theatre spaces will quickly reach this conclusion: Most theatre artists have performed and presented plays in venues as impressive as the Albert Hall in London and as humble as a stack of wooden pallets in a public parking lot. Theatre happens everywhere, and the lavishness of the location doesn't always reflect the quality of the work presented. There have been some amazing performances on very humble stages. Sometimes the actor faces a few familiar faces and many empty seats, sometime she or he is in Central Park relating to thousands of people. Every space, every individual theatre, carries with it advantages as well as challenges to the theatrical company. All of that said, there are a few classic types of theatres and stage designs that any student leaving an Intro to Theatre class should be familiar with, not just for architectural reasons but for the advantages and challenges each type of space presents to the artists.

the proscenium theatre

# 11: the theatre space/the stage

This style of theatre space is most likely the first image that enters an American audience member's mind when they are asked, "What is a theatre?" The word *proscenium* is a Latin word meaning "in front of the scenery," and its use goes back to the **Roman Theatre** circa 240 BCE to the time of the Fall of Rome, which occurred in the year 476 AD. Paradoxically, although the word proscenium was coined during Roman times, there were no proscenium theatres in use or even designed during that era. In modern parlance, proscenium is more of a reference to the arch that covers the edge of the acting area in such a theatre. This proscenium arch separates the stage area from the audience area and essentially frames the picture that is occurring onstage. Proscenium theatres began appearing in western Europe during the late 1500s, and there is some debate as to which specific space is indeed the oldest surviving Proscenium theatre. Many scholars do agree that it was possibly the **Teatro Farnese** in Parma, Italy, which was built in 1618 by Giovanni Battista Aleotti. That theatre was almost destroyed by an Allied air raid during World War Two. It was rebuilt and reopened in 1962. This space is claimed to be the first of the design although, ironically, when the theatre was first built, plays were not performed there. (1,2)

Proscenium theatres tend to create a two-dimensional aspect to the viewer—they are like looking into a painting or a television screen to an extent—and therefore the actors and the director have to be aware of this so as to be sure they create blocking and actions that enhance the physical depth of the scene. This is one of the challenges of this type of space. The designers also can help give the proscenium stage depth and perspective by creating multiple levels, acting areas on platforms or ramps, or any number of techniques. The lighting designer also can do many things to enhance depth and three-dimensionality to the viewer. One of the advantages of a proscenium theatre is that the framing effect of the arch creates a pleasing visual aesthetic in the same way the frame makes a painting seem complete. The arch focuses your eyes, naturally, to the stage area. Figuratively, it says, "Look inside this frame, this is where the story is happening." Proscenium stages also tend to enhance the sense of the 4th Wall; the defined end of the stage combined with the overhead arch makes a flat plane in space that the audience, through a mild form of optical illusion, perceives as a transparent division between the seats and the acting area.

## the thrust stage/theatre

Thrust stages are also a very common layout found in modern theatres. Simply put, a **Thrust Stage** juts out past the edge of the acting area provided by a proscenium stage. This platform creates a situation where audience members are looking on from three sides; one group looking straight on to the action, one group looking from the left side of the house, and one group looking from the right. Thrust stages come right into the audience area, although they generally remain separate from the seating through elevation of the stage or some other form of spatial distinction. This arrangement, of course, provides challenges and advantages as well to the actors, director, and designers. The presence of the audience on three sides presents, suddenly, a distinct sightline issue. If a viewer looks at the action from the right or the left, he or she will occasionally find themselves without visual access to an actor's face. Characters will occasionally have their backs to part of the crowd. The director must be aware of this. She or he must make the blocking more kinetic than might be necessary in a proscenium setting. People have to move so that the audience is given, as much as possible, equal visual access to the important moments in the play. An added aesthetic layer is this: that movement cannot simply be arbitrary. Those kinetic moments where the picture flips for the benefit of the audience have to be justified by the actor and director. A character cannot just move for the sake of moving. That movement must have a distinct purpose that fits the character and the needs of the scene. A director may tell an actor, "Please cross upstage right on this line," and that direction may be largely related to cleaning the stage picture, but that actor has to come up with some meaningful action that brings her or him to that upstage right position. Among the advantages of a thrust stage, the most significant is this:

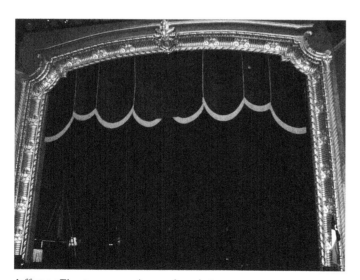

*Jefferson Theatre proscenium arch and stage.*

Suddenly, the actors are *out there in the audience area, without the framing of the proscenium that might tend to make a performance less accessible*. In other words, a thrust stage provides a greater opportunity (or at least an easier opportunity physically) for a sense of *intimacy between audience and actor*. People aren't separated by a straight-edged stage apron; they are among each other. Audience members in a thrust stage situation might now not only be watching the play from different perspectives, they quite often find themselves in a situation where they see both the actors onstage and audience members on the other side. During a powerful scene, you, the watcher, might see the agony not only on a character's face but the reaction of a total stranger in a different seat across from you to that character's agony.

*Arles Roman theater pillar ruins*

## theatre in the round/arena theatres

Although intrinsically different in geometric shape, a theatre in the round or an arena stage presents a play in similar ways and with similar advantages/challenges to the director, designers, and actors. Arena stages feature seating in a square around the stage/acting area. In general, unlike thrust and proscenium situations, the audience is raked upward from a stage that is on the floor of the space. The stage isn't elevated, those watching the show are. Theatre in the round features a circular seating area looking into the acting area, again, in most cases from above. The challenge with the audience sightline becomes much larger here for the actors and the director. The simple fact is this: With the audience on all sides of the stage, it cannot be avoided that from time to time an actor's back will be to the seats during an important moment of the play. The use of motion, kinetic action onstage to shift perspective, is again an approach to balancing the issue, but it is no panacea. An audience member might look into Willy Loman's face and see him shout, "A man is not a piece of fruit!" and that moment will shape the entire evening for that audience member. She will forever remember that night's performance and talk about that horrible anguished pain that she saw in Willie's eyes at that moment and see it as the transformative beat of the entire play. If that audience member has a friend seeing the play on the same night, and that friend has a seat that faces Willy's back at that precise moment of the same show, that second audience member hears the same line shouted, but her impression will be shaped by watching the reaction of the character he shouts it to. That character, Howard Wagner, is Willy's boss and he is 25 years younger than Willy. Howard Wagner is a very cold man who, by the end of the scene, actually fires Willy; he is a cruel man who has used Willy up and, in fact, treated him like a piece of fruit. The second audience member, the one who sees Willy's back and Howard Wagner's face, *has seen precisely the same moment of precisely the same performance*, but her impression of this electrically charged beat will not be based upon Willy's pain, it will be based upon Howard Wagner's indifference to it. When the two audience members get together for coffee after the show, they are likely to talk about this Moment and its power within the narrative. Over coffee they might actually feel like the other person totally missed the point or message at that moment, but neither of them is right or wrong. The moment

*2012 Buffalo State production of* Dames at Sea

becomes different to those who watch the play based upon who is within their sight. Essentially, these two friends went to the same theatre on the same night and saw two different versions of the same play at the same time. This is something that a movie cannot do, and it is one of the major artistic differences between film and theatre. A film director can, along with the cinematographer, guarantee you are looking into the face of the actor he or she wants you to see at any given moment. In theatre, the director can only shape the play so much, can only guide the viewer's eye so much, and ultimately, the viewer has more choice in what they watch.

## black box/flexible theatre

A **Black Box** (also commonly called a **Flexible Theatre**) is an adaptable space. The term "Black box" refers to the fact that in most theatres of this design the walls of the space are painted black to give the space neutrality and direct the eyes of the audience to the acting area. The word "box" is used because a great many (but again, not all) flexible theatre spaces are in square rooms. Any indoor space, regardless of its number of walls, can be turned into a black box. What makes it flexible is that, usually, the space has seating that can be moved, and therefore the space can function as an arena stage, a thrust stage, or even a proscenium stage (up to and including building a temporary arch.) Many smaller theatre companies present their shows in black box settings because all the company has to do to create a theatre space is find a room and some paint and some chairs. The term storefront theatre refers to this kind of ingenuity. The theatre company doesn't have to rent out Carnegie Hall; it can acquire an abandoned convenience store, paint the walls, and bolt up some pipes into the ceiling to hold the lights. It is a common low-budget way to present a play, although it must be noted that all over the world there are some black box/flexible stage theatres that are very well appointed with state-of-the-art lighting, seating, and sound.

It bears repeating that the reader can (and hopefully will, as an enthusiastic lifelong theatregoer) find theatre spaces that are so innovative in design that they fit none of the categories described here. The described designs represent the preponderance but not the entirety of architectural forms and possibilities. From the parking lot pallets to whatever new design the reader might find her- or himself sitting and watching a play in a lifetime, the challenge remains the same for the artists. It is the task of the entire creative team to use the advantages and liabilities of the theatre space to the best of their ability. An artist must use the materials available, including the physical environs, to serve the play and its message and convey that message to the ticket buyers who watch.

(1) Kimball King, *Western Drama Through the Ages*.

(2) Paul Kuritz, *The Making of Theatre History*.

S imply stated, the **Playwright** is the person or persons who wrote the play. The readers of this text may collectively roll their eyes when they read that sentence, because it is indeed seemingly obvious on the surface. There is, however, so much more to the creation of the series of written words that become a viable and moving piece of theatre, a "play." The process involves so much more than just sitting down at a desk and writing on a legal pad or typing on a computer keyboard. That is why the author of a play is given the specific term of playwright. Look at the construction of the word itself: "playwright." The spelling seems strange, doesn't it? Why are the letters "g" and "h" there? It has to do with what writing a play actually entails. A wright is someone who works to create something (such as a wheelwright or a shipwright, who design and create, respectively, wheels and ships.) "Wright" describes the craft that goes into the work of creation. It is a great word to meditate on when thinking of the process by which the words that make a play are assembled. Inspiration, talent, intellect, experience, and even what is known romantically as "the Muse" are all aspects of writing a play, but in the end there is also a great deal of craft to it. Creating a dramatic work is

# 12: the play structure

both art and technique. You have probably heard many writers refer to their work as their "baby." The metaphor is quite apt, really. As this chapter of the book unfolds, you will see many similarities between the nurturing of a child from infancy through adolescence up through adulthood and even old age. Plays have points of development—evolutionary moments—that can only be referred to as "maturing," and just like with a baby, it takes time indeed to accomplish. A play can tell a story; in fact, more often than not a play does, but the ultimate choice of how that story is told and what characters appear to live it out in front of the audience falls solely into the hands of the playwright. It is important to note at this point that plays do not necessarily have to tell a story in a linear fashion. Plays have been and are being written with no defined beginning, middle, and end, and we will discuss that in greater depth in later chapters.

For the purposes of understanding the occupation of a playwright, we will focus on the processes that go into the final edition of a script, and in particular upon the dramatic elements that were defined more than two millennia ago by the Greek philosopher and literary critic Aristotle. A typical modern student reads "Greek philosopher and literary critic" and wishes she was still in bed or wonders what this could have to do with writing a play. However, the reader need not know anything about reading Greek in order to understand Aristotle.

In fact, his precepts not only are familiar to anyone who has learned to read and write in English, they are evident in the very structure of this book and each of its chapters. The dramatic story elements that Aristotle defined in his book *Poetics* will be very easy for you to learn and understand. You will understand his elements of storytelling for one simple reason: you already know them. You use Aristotle's concepts daily in your own speech and communication. They are the backbone of almost all storytelling, drama, and literature in Western culture.

Aristotle defined drama as having two distinct genres: **Tragedy** and **Comedy**. The traditional masks of these two genres, the smiling face of comedy next to or even interwoven with the weeping, grimacing face of tragedy is synonymous in all Western culture with these branches of storytelling.

In simplest terms, Aristotle distinguished between tragedy and comedy, using the terms "**Pitiful and Fearful**" to describe the dramatic arc and tension found in a tragedy, while ascribing the term "**Ridiculous**" to describe the plotline of a comedy. The "ridiculous" in Aristotle's nomenclature describes a story whose plot, despite the fault or faults of the protagonist, results in a conclusion that is ultimately neither painful nor destructive to the characters in the play. In short, no unhappy ending equals no tragedy equals comedy.

The "pitiful and fearful" resolution of a classic Aristotlean tragedy refers to the loss and woes that befall characters in a tragic play. In short, this means the ending is unhappy: The Protagonist dies; his or her plans fail; bad luck (up to and including shame, banishment, and quite often the death of many characters, including the protagonist) is the consequence of the protagonist's tragic flaw at the play's end.

Aristotle was not the first to discuss the terms protagonist and antagonist, but these are essential to understanding his definition of drama.

The simplest explanation is that the protagonist is the subject of the story and plotline of a play. The drama of theatre comes from the struggle of the protagonist to achieve his or her goals and desires against the obstacles the character befalls. In tragedy, the protagonist suffers for her or his **Tragic Flaw**, which is also called *Hamartia*.[1] This tragic flaw leads to the downfall of the protagonist in a tragedy. In both tragedy and comedy, the protagonist is the person in the play with whom the audience shares the journey. It is "their story."

Again, in simplest terms, the antagonist is the character or characters in a tragic play who present obstacles that thwart the protagonist in the pursuit of her or his goals. In more complex theatre, the antagonist may, in fact, be something other than an actual human being. The antagonist could be fate, or the gods, or mortality, or even the protagonist's tragic flaw.

An imperfect but acceptably accurate way to describe both characters is to say that the protagonist is the "hero," while the antagonist is the "villain."

---

1   For the most part, *hamartia* literally translates as "fatal flaw," but the word also includes the concept that it is *an injury committed in ignorance*. In other words, the fatal flaw of the protagonist hurts not only him- or herself, it hurts others as well.

Unfortunately, many of Aristotle's actual physical texts were partially lost to the ravages of time. A great deal of his written theories and outlook on comedy has had to be reconstructed through examination of criticism by his contemporaries and ideas inferred from his writings about tragedy.

So let's look at what Aristotle had to say about tragedy. These ideas have had tremendous influence from his time to the present day, and they were the basis of an important theatrical concept that came to be known as "the well-made play," which we will later discuss at length.

In *Poetics*, Aristotle described six elements that he believed to be essential in creating good drama. These elements are:

1.  Plot

2.  Character

3.  Theme

4.  Diction

5.  Music

6.  Spectacle

*Aristotle, Ptolemy, and Copernicus discussing matters of astronomy beneath Medici family ducal crown and banner*

All of these words are very familiar to a modern audience. In fact, they are very familiar to modern people in their day-to-day lives as well. But in theatrical terms, what was Aristotle talking about? Let's look at each term in order.

First, we have the element of **Plot**. From Aristotle's point of view, a play first and foremost has to tell a story. Events must occur over the course of time in which individual characters in the play were affected. For instance, there might be a murder. There might be a plot against the rightful government. A character may use his or her power to steal the love of another character. The plot could be something simple, or it could be as complicated as the tale of *Oedipus*, where a heroic man is undone by the fact that he has unwittingly killed his father and become intimate with his own mother (through a series of convoluted murders, intrigues, and political conspiracies).

In Aristotle's view, the second element, **Character**, involves a dramatic artifice known as the tragic flaw. In a tragedy, Aristotle posited, the protagonist (the main character of the play) may be a man or woman of great virtue, bravery, and wisdom. Nevertheless, this tragic hero is ultimately undone by his or her tragic flaw/**Hamartia**. Hamartia, or the tragic flaw, is a trait possessed by the character that involves the weaknesses of human nature. Examples of these flaws are rage, greed, lust, and many others, the foremost of which is hubris. Hubris refers to the ultimate form of pride—the pride that can make a human believe she is above or not subject to the laws of the gods or the Fates. Hubris leads a mortal to believe he is on an equal level with the gods. In the world of Aristotle, where plays were very often incorporated into religious worship and ritual, a mortal placing himself on the level of a deity is the ultimate and most unforgivable sin. Hubris is, of course, not the only potential tragic flaw. Rage, jealousy, greed, and lust (in fact, all of the traditional Seven Deadly Sins) are potential tragic flaws for a playwright to imbue their protagonist with. One of the tenets of Aristotle's definition of tragedy was that the protagonist realizes before the play is over what her or his tragic flaw is, but this does not save the protagonist from destruction. Knowing your tragic flaw is not enough; the punishment of the gods is not open to appeal anymore. This reflects the general religious thinking of the time as well. The gods of Greece and Rome were not gods of redemption. For the most part, redemption is a concept that came into literature after the rise of Christianity, at least in Western culture.

Element three, **Theme**, concerns what we would now refer to as the "**Message**" of the play. Once again, it is important to note that Greek drama was frequently integrated into religious ritual. The preeminent themes of Aristotle's time concerned themselves with the desires and demands of the gods. Theme relates to an overall message that the **Rules of the Gods** were righteous and that human beings who possessed true virtue followed the commands of the gods. Morally speaking, a play is expected to demonstrate that certain ideals always hold true, such as the **Triumph of Good** and the **Inevitability of Fate**.

Element four is **Diction.** This refers not only to clarity of speech and projection (although more often than not, actors in ancient Greek drama were speaking on outdoor stages through masks that were designed to indicate their emotional state while covering their faces) but also the actor's use of speech to convey the societal status and moral condition of her or his character. Therefore, a noble character would be expected to speak in a tone and with a clarity that conveyed not just emotion but a state of intrinsic high status and education within the character. A lower, or "base," character would endeavor to sound less elevated in education, honesty, and dignity. Aristotle's definition of diction also was a technical one as well. He believed that it was important for actors to stress consonants while speaking on stage to enhance clarity; he believed that playwrights were charged with the task of choosing words whose consonants would aid the actors in sounding both clear and poetic to the audience. Diction was no small consideration when relating to an audience while talking through masks with no ceilings or walls to enhance acoustics. These were formidable challenges to both performers and playwrights alike.

The fifth element in Aristotle's description is **Music**. Greek drama frequently utilizes a chorus which would comment on as well as participate in the action. The chorus sang many of their lines (in some plays and performances, they sang all of their lines). Aristotle believed that musical accompaniment was integral to establishing and enhancing mood, which complemented the tenor of the scenes.

The sixth and final element of drama as espoused in Aristotle's *Poetics* is **Spectacle**.[2] The presentation of the story, especially scenes of violence or interference by the gods, must be

---

2   Spectacle is a very big part of modern theatre, especially in the world of musicals. Many shows these days feature spectacular pyrotechnics (à la *Spider-Man* and *Wicked*), large sculpted sets and costume pieces (such as the **Parade of Animals** in *The Lion King*), laser lighting effects (*The Gazillion Bubble Show*), and sound effects

presented in a fashion which leaves the audience in awe. If a king is murdered, there must be many people on stage to witness and be affected by it. If the gods chose to intervene, they would enter dramatically and spectacularly, often descending to the stage in a basket or small platform that was swung onto the stage by the use of a crane behind or at the side of the stage. This descent from the heavens to rectify the world or enforce the justice of the immortals was referred to as **Deus Ex Machina,** which translates into modern English as "God in the machine." (Today, not only in theatre but in all literature, Deus Ex Machina refers to any plot device which arrives at the last moment to fix whatever has happened in the story at the very end. The Cavalry arriving in an old western movie just as the heroes were about to be overrun by their enemies is a classic case of Deus Ex Machina, as was the arrival of Rudolph with his shiny nose on Christmas Eve as the inclement weather threatened the postponement of Christmas. Dorothy awakening at the end of *The Wizard of Oz* to find her adventure was all a dream was a subtle literary and dramatic form of Deus Ex Machina as well.) Simply stated, "spectacle" means that the drama inherent in a tragedy had to be more than emotionally stirring—it had to be visually stunning as well.

Like most writers, Aristotle was influenced not only by his time but modern times as well, by the orally handed down writings of Homer. Long after Homer's death, these stories, along with other epic poems from the oral tradition created by different storytellers, were finally written down and can be read in multiple translations today. Homer's great lyric poems, *The Iliad* and *The Odyssey*, introduced a form of dramatic storytelling in which a story would have a beginning, a middle, and an end. The protagonist would face many challenges in trying to accomplish his goals, and, in fact, might even die in the process of pursuing them. This is how we tell stories for the most part today, even true anecdotes from our lives. We set the scene, define the good and bad guys in our story, describe what the good guys went through, and ultimately conclude with how it all ended. Aristotle gave this format to theatre. He described the need for a play to have several aspects to be well written. In much later times, notably the 18th and 19th centuries, these story elements became defined as the essentials to creating what was termed a "**Well Made Play**."

Taking the lead from Aristotle, a properly structured play generally adhered to this format.

1. Exposition

2. Introduction of Conflict

3. Inciting Incident

4. Rising Action/Plot Complication

5. Climax/Catharsis

6. Denouement/End of the play/Resolution

_____

made newly possible and very affordable by advances in technology (featured in almost all modern Broadway shows, from *Shrek* to *Rock of Ages*.)

Let's quickly define these terms.

Exposition refers to the words and actions delivered by the characters in a play that let us know what we are watching. They include the Who, What, Where, When, and Why of the show. The prevalent approach taken by playwrights (although not always, of course) is to include as much information about these five w's in the early part of the script. The playwright more often than not wants to get that information out there and out of the way so that she or he can get on with the actual storytelling. Modern audiences of theatre, film, and television are so used to this "expository information" that often we do not notice it. The very first few scenes in a play or film usually contain simple information. Expository information continually comes out throughout a play, and a good example of this is to look at any kind of murder mystery. The single most important piece of expository information ("Whodunit?") is usually withheld from the audience until the very end.

Introduction of Conflict is the point, usually early in the text, where the audience finds out the emotional and life circumstances that are creating tension between the characters in the play. Conflict in Aristotelean theatre is a necessity: the characters not only must have obstacles facing them personally, they also need to have other characters whose desires and needs work against achieving their goals.

The Inciting Incident is often called as the introduction of "Action." Something has to happen—there has to be an incident, a tangible event such as a murder or a romantic connection between characters that plays out on the stage. The assassination of Caesar in Shakespeare's *Julius Caesar* is an inciting incident. It leads to civil war and the end of Brutus and his allies.

Rising action/plot complication is a way to describe what also is referred to in modern times as "build." The events begin to move faster within the narrative because the inciting incident begins a snowball of reaction. Mark Antony's speech in *Julius Caesar*, "They are all honorable men," does this. The murders of Mercutio and Tybalt in *Romeo and Juliet* do this. The plot gets complicated because events are moving too fast and the life of the protagonist (especially, again, in tragedy) is moving too fast for him or her to keep up with.

Climax/Catharsis is the point in a play where the story comes to its highest emotional point. The narrative of the script, the characters, and most importantly, the audience, cannot take any more tension or emotion. Events, either active events like Romeo poisoning himself or emotional events like when Garcin shouts "Hell is other people!" in Jean-Paul Sartre's *No Exit*, come to a head. All the secrets have been revealed, and the audience and characters onstage can release their emotions in what Aristotle defined as catharsis. Aristotle saw catharsis as a "Purification" or "Purgation" of emotion, a complete release of feeling that allows the audience to fully feel the weight of the play. For all intents and purposes, the actual story has ended, but Aristotle believed that there was one more thing necessary—denouement or resolution.

Simply stated, denouement is the tying up of loose ends within the play. The playwright at this point is charged with the task of giving the audience explanations of what happens to the characters and the world of the play after the story ends. Hidden motives that led to the climax may be revealed. Characters may talk about where they plan to go, about "moving on," or seeking revenge at a later date. Every child whose mother has said, "And they all lived happily ever after," at the end of a bedtime story understands denouement. It is what we need to know to let the story end and leave the theatre feeling that the plot has no (or as few as possible) holes in it. Resolution is also a good description, and this is indeed the point that is the end of the play.

## Explanation of terms using *Death of a Salesman*

**Exposition** is an area that tests the craft of a playwright. Using dialogue from your characters, how do you naturally introduce the information that gives the storyline its foundation, in a way that is believable and subtle? Let's use the classic Arthur Miller drama *Death of a Salesman* as a template. In *Death of a Salesman*, we meet Willy Loman, a salesman in his early sixties whose life is falling apart and his health is deteriorating. We also meet his extremely devoted and practical wife, Linda Loman, as well as their sons, Biff and Happy. Biff and Happy are in their thirties and are troubled by a great number of issues, not the least of which is that they constantly lie about their lives, relationships, and career success. Specifically, in the early parts of the play, we learn that Biff is particularly troubled and has returned home after a long absence to start again his life in Brooklyn. As the story unfolds, we find that Biff was Willy's favorite son and that Willy vicariously lived through Biff when Biff was a high school football star. But something has happened. At the beginning of the play, we get hints but the issue slowly reveals itself until at the end of the play we are overwhelmed by several tragic events.

So the beginning of the play has a great many details to give the audience that it will need to care emotionally and follow the trajectory of the play. This is exposition, and those details are known as expository information. Arthur Miller does a particularly marvelous job in the opening scene of weaving the expository information into believable and active dialogue. The entire scene is expository by definition, but we have certain remarkable moments of information that are delivered seamlessly within a completely believable section of dialogue. The most classic exposition lines will be numbered and discussed at the end of this excerpt. What is exposition? Let's look at the first few pages of the play and see.

> Willy Loman, the salesman, enters, carrying two large sample cases. The flute plays on. He hears but is not *aware of it. He is past sixty years of age, dressed quietly. Even as he crosses the stage to the doorway of the house, his exhaustion is apparent. He unlocks the door, comes into the kitchen, and thankfully lets his burden down, feeling the soreness of his palms. A word-sigh escapes his lips—it might be "Oh, boy, oh, boy." He closes the door, then carries his cases out into the living room, through the draped kitchen doorway. Linda, his wife, has stirred in her bed at the right. She gets out and puts on a robe, listening.*
>
> LINDA *(hearing Willy outside the bedroom, calls with some trepidation)*: Willy!
>
> WILLY: It's all right. I came back.

LINDA: Why? What happened? *(Slight pause.)* Did something happen, Willy?

WILLY: No, nothing happened.

LINDA: You didn't smash the car, did you? (1)

WILLY *(with casual irritation)*: I said nothing happened. Didn't you hear me?

LINDA: Don't you feel well?

WILLY: I'm tired to the death. (2) *(The flute has faded away. He sits on the bed beside her, a little numb.)* I couldn't make it. I just couldn't make it, Linda.

LINDA *(very carefully, delicately)*: Where were you all day? You look terrible.

WILLY: I got as far as a little above Yonkers. I stopped for a cup of coffee. Maybe it was the coffee. (3)

LINDA: What?

WILLY *(after a pause)*: I suddenly couldn't drive any more. The car kept going off onto the shoulder, y'know?

LINDA *(helpfully)*: Oh. Maybe it was the steering again. I don't think Angelo knows the Studebaker.

WILLY: No, it's me, it's me. Suddenly I realize I'm goin' sixty miles an hour and I don't remember the last five minutes. I'm—I can't seem to—keep my mind to it. (4)

LINDA: Maybe it's your glasses. You never went for your new glasses.

WILLY: No, I see everything. I came back ten miles an hour. It took me nearly four hours from Yonkers.

LINDA *(resigned)*: Well, you'll just have to take a rest, Willy, you can't continue this way.

WILLY: I just got back from Florida.

LINDA: But you didn't rest your mind. Your mind is overactive, and the mind is what counts, dear.

WILLY: I'll start out in the morning. Maybe I'll feel better in the morning. *(She is taking off his shoes.)* These goddam arch supports are killing me.

LINDA: Take an aspirin. Should I get you an aspirin? It'll soothe you.

WILLY (with wonder): I was driving along, you understand? And I was fine. I was even observing the scenery. You can imagine, me looking at scenery, on the road every week of my life. (5) But it's so beautiful up there, Linda, the trees are so thick, and the sun is warm. I opened the windshield and just let the warm air bathe over me. And then all of a sudden I'm goin' off the road! I'm tellin' ya, I absolutely forgot I was driving. If I'd've gone the other way over the white line I might've killed somebody. So I went on again—and five minutes later I'm dreamin' again, and I nearly ... (He presses two fingers against his eyes.) I have such thoughts, I have such strange thoughts. (6)

LINDA: Willy, dear. Talk to them again. There's no reason why you can't work in New York.

WILLY: They don't need me in New York. I'm the New England man. I'm vital in New England.

LINDA: But you're sixty years old. They can't expect you to keep travelling every week. (7)

WILLY: I'll have to send a wire to Portland. I'm supposed to see Brown and Morrison tomorrow morning at ten o'clock to show the line. Goddammit, I could sell them! (He starts putting on his jacket.)

LINDA (taking the jacket from him): Why don't you go down to the place tomorrow and tell Howard you've simply got to work in New York? You're too accommodating, dear.

WILLY: If old man Wagner was alive I'd a been in charge of New York now! That man was a prince, he was a masterful man.

But that boy of his, that Howard, he don't appreciate. When I went north the first time, the Wagner Company didn't know where New England was! (8)

LINDA: Why don't you tell those things to Howard, dear?

WILLY (encouraged): I will, I definitely will. Is there any cheese?

LINDA: I'll make you a sandwich.

WILLY: No, go to sleep. I'll take some milk. I'll be up right away. The boys in? (9)

LINDA: They're sleeping. Happy took Biff on a date tonight.

WILLY (interested): That so?

LINDA: It was so nice to see them shaving together, one behind the other, in the bathroom. And going out together. You notice? The whole house smells of shaving lotion.

WILLY: Figure it out. Work a lifetime to pay off a house. You finally own it, and there's nobody to live in it.

LINDA: Well, dear, life is a casting off. It's always that way.

WILLY: No, no, some people—some people accomplish something. Did Biff say anything after I went this morning?

LINDA: You shouldn't have criticised him, Willy, especially after he just got off the train. You mustn't lose your temper with him. (10)

WILLY: When the hell did I lose my temper? I simply asked him if he was making any money. Is that a criticism?

LINDA: But, dear, how could he make any money?

WILLY (worried and angered): There's such an undercurrent in him. He became a moody man. Did he apologize when I left this morning?

LINDA: He was crestfallen, Willy. You know how he admires you. I think if he finds himself, then you'll both be happier and not fight any more.

WILLY: How can he find himself on a farm? Is that a life? A farmhand? In the beginning, when he was young, I thought, well, a young man, it's good for him to tramp around, take a lot of different jobs. But it's more than ten years now and he has yet to make thirty-five dollars a week! (11)

LINDA: He's finding himself, Willy.

WILLY: Not finding yourself at the age of thirty-four is a disgrace! (12)

LINDA: Shh!

WILLY: The trouble is he's lazy, goddammit!

LINDA: Willy, please!

WILLY: Biff is a lazy bum! (13-A)

LINDA: They're sleeping. Get something to eat. Go on down.

WILLY: Why did he come home? I would like to know what brought him home.

LINDA: I don't know. I think he's still lost, Willy. I think he's very lost.

WILLY: Biff Loman is lost. In the greatest country in the world a young man with such—personal attractiveness, gets lost. And such a hard worker. There's one thing about Biff—he's not lazy. (13-B)

LINDA: Never.

WILLY (*with pity and resolve*): I'll see him in the morning; I'll have a nice talk with him. I'll get him a job selling. He could be big in no time. My God! Remember how they used to follow him around in high school? When he smiled at one of them their faces lit up. When he walked down the street … (14) (*He loses himself in reminiscences.*)

The dialogue in this scene is simple, elegant, truthful, and absolutely believable. It is a realistic exchange between a couple who have been married many years. But look at the numbered sections and all that we've been told by the playwright within this naturalistic talk! Here's what we learned, just in those footnoted and numbered lines and words.

1.  Linda worries that Willy smashed the car. This line clearly implies that she's afraid he has smashed it again.

2.  Willy says he is tired, but not just "bad day tired"; he is tired to the death. Here we begin to learn that his weariness and depression are profound, and this is only eight lines into the play.

3.  Willy got as far as Yonkers, which is not very far from Brooklyn. This is basic "story" info but it sets up the other emotional issues of the scene.

4.  Willy is losing concentration and memory, even as he drives his car at 60 miles per hour. We learn here that he is not only tired and depressed, he is beginning to face real danger due to his physical and cognitive loss.

5.  Quite naturally, we are told by Willy that he has "been on the road every week of my life." We get to see the source of the weariness without noticing the artifice of the author.

6.  "I have such strange thoughts." In an intimate plea to his wife we, the audience, are allowed to know that Willy is emotionally troubled and doesn't understand his thoughts. "Strange" is a wonderful choice of adjective here. It implies that these thoughts are new and not understood by Willy. It tells us a great deal with just one single-syllable word.

7.  "You're sixty years old. They can't expect you to keep travelling every week." The love of a wife is contained in this line, and her deep concern for her husband's health. But more directly, we learn that Willy is 60 and travels every week, which confirms Willy's earlier observation that he's been on the road all of his life. This is straight up 5W information—again, it is seamlessly woven into a real scene between believable characters.

8.  This entire speech, ending in Willy's complaint that the new boss doesn't even know the business or the territories, lets us in, very organically, into the resentments that Willy is feeling toward his occupation and lifestyle.

9.  "The boys in?" Arthur Miller switches the subject conceptually while simultaneously introducing new characters, "the boys," who we now can hear described by their parents before we even meet them.

10. "You shouldn't have criticised him Willy, especially after he just got off the train. You mustn't lose your temper with him." Here we learn, in a tender chiding exchange between Linda and her husband, that Biff just got off a train (and therefore has arrived from somewhere other than Brooklyn) and that Willy lost his temper with him. We know that Willy and Biff are fighting even before we see them do it. We know that Willy shows his temper with his son when he comes to the house, at least in this one foreshadowing instance.

11. "It's more than ten years now and he has yet to make thirty-five dollars a week!" Through Willy, we are learning biographical facts about Biff here. Biff has been working for at least ten years, and he is not doing very well financially. We also begin to learn that Willy defines success as something with a specific monetary value.

12. "Not finding yourself at the age of thirty-four is a disgrace!!!" Biff is 34.

13. A and 13-B. Arthur Miller wants us to know that Willy's moods, and even his perspective of what is happening or true, is in flux. Willy doesn't know, or perhaps keep track, of the fact that his statements contradict each other in very short order. The passage containing 13-A is one clearly damning assessment of his son, Biff: he's a lazy bum. The line noted by 13-B has Willy saying this: "There's one thing about Biff—He's not lazy." These two statements are diametrically opposing opinions, and they are separated from each other by only 70 words of dialogue between Willy and Linda! If you take Linda's words out of the passage, we find that, between saying, "Biff is a lazy bum" and "he's not lazy," Willy only speaks 44 words. It is an amazing turnaround and gives the audience a mountain of insight into this particular salesman, while also providing a very good moment of humor in a play that needs laughter occasionally to balance the pain of the narrative.

Introduction of conflict is essential for a story to move. If everyone in the play gets along and has no problems, it is very hard to make an audience stay interested. In *Death of a Salesman*, we are given many flashbacks in time, and during these flashbacks the events and choices that Willy and the family have made explain to us and introduce us to what the problem is now. The very first traveling we do, going back into the Loman family history, is to a scene from Biff's high school days when he was a big star and highly admired. But something is amiss. Willy lets some things go in the scene that are indeed the core of the conflict he has with his sons now that they are adults. Let's examine the dialogue. Remember, Willy is speaking at age 60 but talking to his boys aloud when they were teens:

> *(Willy is gradually addressing—physically—a point offstage, speaking through the wall of the kitchen, and his voice has been rising in volume to that of a normal conversation.)*

WILLY: I been wondering why you polish the car so careful. Ha!

Don't leave the hubcaps, boys. Get the chamois to the hubcaps.

Happy, use newspaper on the windows, it's the easiest thing.

Show him how to do it Biff! You see, Happy? Pad it up, use it like a pad. That's it, that's it, good work. You're doin' all right, Hap. *(He pauses, then nods in approbation for a few seconds, then looks upward.)* Biff, first thing we gotta do when we get time is clip that big branch over the house. Afraid it's gonna fall in a storm and hit the roof. Tell you what. We get a rope and sling her around, and then we climb up there with a couple of saws and take her down. Soon as you finish the car, boys, I wanna see ya. I got a surprise for you, boys.

BIFF *(offstage)*: Whatta ya got, Dad?

WILLY: No, you finish first. Never leave a job till you're finished—remember that. (1) *(Looking toward the "big trees".)* Biff, up in Albany I saw a beautiful hammock. I think I'll buy it next trip, and we'll hang it right between those two elms. Wouldn't that be something? Just swingin' there under those branches. Boy, that would be …

*(Young Biff and Young Happy appear from the direction Willy was addressing. Happy carries rags and a pail of water. Biff, wearing a sweater with a block "S", carries a football.)*

BIFF *(pointing in the direction of the car offstage)*: How's that, Pop, professional?

WILLY: Terrific. Terrific job, boys. Good work, Biff.

HAPPY: Where's the surprise, Pop?

WILLY: In the back seat of the car.

HAPPY: Boy! *(He runs off.)*

BIFF: What is it, Dad? Tell me, what'd you buy?

WILLY *(laughing, cuffs him)*: Never mind, something I want you to have.

BIFF *(turns and starts off)*: What is it, Hap?

HAPPY *(offstage)*: It's a punching bag!

BIFF: Oh, Pop!

WILLY: It's got Gene Tunney's signature on it! *(Happy runs onstage with a punching bag.)*

BIFF: Gee, how'd you know we wanted a punching bag?

WILLY: Well, it's the finest thing for the timing.

HAPPY *(lies down on his back and pedals with his feet)*: I'm losing weight, you notice, Pop? (2)

WILLY *(to Happy)*: Jumping rope is good too.

BIFF: Did you see the new football I got?

WILLY *(examining the ball)*: Where'd you get a new ball?

BIFF: The coach told me to practice my passing.

WILLY: That so? And he gave you the ball, heh?

BIFF: Well, I borrowed it from the locker room. *(He laughs confidentially.)* (3)

WILLY *(laughing with him at the theft)*: I want you to return that. (4)

HAPPY: I told you he wouldn't like it! (5)

BIFF *(angrily)*: Well, I'm bringing it back! (6)

WILLY *(stopping the incipient argument, to Happy)*: Sure, he's gotta practice with a regulation ball, doesn't he? *(To Biff.)*

Coach'll probably congratulate you on your initiative! (7)

BIFF: Oh, he keeps congratulating my initiative all the time, Pop. (8)

WILLY: That's because he likes you. If somebody else took that ball there'd be an uproar. (9)

This scene shows us, in vivid detail, the warped ideals and conflicting moralities that Willy holds and imparts to his boys. This is one of many scenes where "introduction of conflict" in this play arguably begins, but given the theme of the play in general—The American Dream—what is being played out here is a perversion of what parenting should be. Let's look at the numbered lines.

1.   "Never leave a job till you're finished—remember that." Willy sounds like the ideal father giving out solid advice to his sons about the value of good work. This is Willy demonstrating his integrity and commitment to values. This commitment doesn't even last through the next ten lines.

2.  "I'm losing weight, you notice, Pop?" Happy is the classic second son; he craves the attention Biff gets without even trying. Later in the play, we see how this interior intellectual conflict plays out in a direct betrayal of his father at a restaurant. Happy literally abandons Willy in the heart of Manhattan, leaving his "Pop" so he can seduce a woman he just met.

3.  "Well, I borrowed it from the locker room." This is a lie, and not the first of Biff's lies. Stealing is a core issue with him, and this section shows us how he was caught red-handed. This is where Willy's values should shine, and he should correct his son.

4.  "I want you to return that." Willy corrects Biff. Or does he? He's laughing. He doesn't demand the ball be immediately returned, he suggests no punishment or restitution. He laughs at his son's entitlement.

5.  "I told you he wouldn't like it!" Happy ditches Biff here, and also tattles on him. There is rivalry that conflicts with the happy reunion between their adult selves, which we just witnessed in the scene before. Once again, Happy lets us know he's not against ditching a family member when that person is inconvenient.

6.  "Well, I'm bringing it back!" You'd once again expect Willy, the man with the integrity, to put a timeframe on this. He doesn't. This is part of a pattern of conflict in Biff's life and his relationship with his father that we see throughout the ensuing scenes.

7.  "Sure, he's gotta practice with a regulation ball, doesn't he? Coach'll probably congratulate you on your initiative!" Willy talks about the stolen ball, then drops the metaphorical ball terribly here. This is an inexcusable message to give your teenage son—that his needs justify theft and that he is to be praised for breaking the rules when it suits him. It is very unlikely his coach will congratulate him, so why does Willy say this? Footnotes 8 and 9 reveal this, and they introduce the conflict that has led Biff back to his father's tiny Brooklyn house as a grown man in his mid thirties.

8.  "Oh, he keeps congratulating my initiative all the time, Pop." Any sensible parent would see that as an immature lie, and any truly compassionate parent would demand better character in her or his kid.

9.  "That's because he likes you. If somebody else took that ball there'd be an uproar."

Because he likes you. This phrase destroys Biff as a man and leads Willy to suicide. Willy would rather be liked by his sons than discipline them. In the end, this is his true failure with Biff, Happy, and Linda. Even faced with his teenage son's larceny, Willy tries to be more friend than dad and in the process creates a pair of men, Biff and Happy, who resent him and disappoint him at every turn. This is what internal conflict means to an actor, director, and playwright. There are other kinds of conflict, including physical acts, which a playwright can and often does use to get the story of a play into kinetic motion. Here, in flashback, we see Arthur Miller show his audience that the conflict isn't a physical fight: It is a denial of the truth.

The inciting incident in *Salesman* is not one single event per se, although the first of these incidents, the one that leads to the destruction at the end of the play, can be seen in another section of the Biff/Happy flashback when Linda comes into the picture. Linda is a woman of practicality and strength who holds Willy and her family together. She always has. Willy's issues with loyalty to Linda on the road (and again his double-talk when it comes to values and integrity) appear as he drifts into a flashback within the flashback. On the road, Willy has been unfaithful. This incident ultimately destroys his family not because Linda finds out (we never know in the text if she does or doesn't, and that's an interesting choice the director and actor have to make when producing the play), but because Biff, as an immature and spoiled teenager, does. In his immaturity, he throws his future away. Here's how we find out about this incident—the inciting moment of information and the event that changes everything forever. In this scene, we also hear from Bernard, Biff's childhood best friend, and his news about what Biff is doing and becoming tells us that things have been unraveling for quite a while. Again, the idea of the inciting incident is not necessarily a single, absolute moment within a text; it can be a series of incidents that add into a pattern.

LINDA: Willy, darling, you're the handsomest man in the world …

WILLY: Oh, no, Linda.

LINDA: To me you are. *(Slight pause.)* The handsomest.

*(From the darkness is heard the laughter of a woman. Willy doesn't turn to it, but it continues through Linda's lines.)*

LINDA: And the boys, Willy. Few men are idolized by their children the way you are.

*(Music is heard as behind a scrim, to the left of the house; The Woman, dimly seen, is dressing.)*

WILLY *(with great feeling)*: You're the best there is, Linda, you're a pal, you know that? On the road—on the road I want to grab you sometimes and just kiss the life outa you. (1)

*(The laughter is loud now, and he moves into a brightening area at the left, where The Woman has come from behind the scrim and is standing, putting on her hat, looking into a "mirror" and laughing.)*

WILLY: Cause I get so lonely—especially when business is bad and there's nobody to talk to. I get the feeling that I'll never sell anything again, that I won't make a living for you, or a business, a business for the boys. *(He talks through The Woman's subsiding laughter; The Woman primps at the "mirror."*

There's so much I want to make for … (2)

THE WOMAN: Me? You didn't make me, Willy. I picked you.

WILLY (pleased): You picked me?

THE WOMAN: (who is quite proper-looking, Willy's age): I did.

I've been sitting at that desk watching all the salesmen go by, day in, day out. But you've got such a sense of humor, and we do have such a good time together, don't we?

WILLY: Sure, sure. (He takes her in his arms.) Why do you have to go now?

THE WOMAN: It's two o'clock …

WILLY: No, come on in! (He pulls her.)

THE WOMAN: … my sisters'll be scandalized. When'll you be back?

WILLY: Oh, two weeks about. Will you come up again?

THE WOMAN: Sure thing. You do make me laugh. It's good for me. (She squeezes his arm, kisses him.) And I think you're a wonderful man.

WILLY: You picked me, heh? (3)

THE WOMAN: Sure. Because you're so sweet. And such a kidder.

WILLY: Well, I'll see you next time I'm in Boston.

THE WOMAN: I'll put you right through to the buyers.

WILLY (slapping her bottom): Right. Well, bottoms up! (4)

THE WOMAN (slaps him gently and laughs): You just kill me, (He suddenly grabs her and kisses her roughly.) You kill me. And thanks for the stockings. I love a lot of stockings. Well, good night. (5)

WILLY: Good night. And keep your pores open!

THE WOMAN: Oh, Willy!

(The Woman bursts out laughing, and Linda's laughter blends in. The Woman disappears into the dark. Now the area at the kitchen table brightens. Linda is sitting where she was at the kitchen table, but now is mending a pair of her silk stockings.)

LINDA: You are, Willy. The handsomest man. You've got no reason to feel that …

WILLY (coming out of The Woman's dimming area and going over to Linda): I'll make it all up to you, Linda, I'll … (6)

LINDA: There's nothing to make up, dear. You're doing fine, better than …

WILLY (noticing her mending): What's that?

LINDA: Just mending my stockings. They're so expensive …

WILLY (angrily, taking them from her): I won't have you mending stockings in this house! Now throw them out! (Linda puts the stockings in her pocket.) (7)

BERNARD (entering on the run): Where is he? If he doesn't study!

WILLY (moving to the forestage, with great agitation): You'll give him the answers! (8)

BERNARD: I do, but I can't on a Regents! That's a state exam!

They're liable to arrest me!

WILLY: Where is he? I'll whip him, I'll whip him!

LINDA: And he'd better give back that football, Willy, it's not nice.

WILLY: Biff! Where is he? Why is he taking everything?

LINDA: He's too rough with the girls, Willy. All the mothers are afraid of him! (9)

WILLY: I'll whip him!

BERNARD: He's driving the car without a license!

(The Woman's laugh is heard.) (10)

WILLY: Shut up!

LINDA: All the mothers …

WILLY: Shut up!

BERNARD (backing quietly away and out): Mr. Birnbaum says he's stuck up.

WILLY: Get outa here!

BERNARD: If he doesn't buckle down he'll flunk math! (He goes off.)

LINDA: He's right, Willy, you've gotta …

WILLY *(exploding at her)*: There's nothing the matter with him!

You want him to be a worm like Bernard? (11) He's got spirit, personality.

*(As he speaks, Linda, almost in tears, exits into the living room. Willy is alone in the kitchen, wilting and staring. The leaves are gone. It is night again, and the apartment houses look down from behind.)*

WILLY: Loaded with it. Loaded! What is he stealing? He's giving it back, isn't he? Why is he stealing? What did I tell him? I never in my life told him anything but decent things. (12)

It is easy to see that something went very wrong on the day of this particular flashback. The audience experiences what is called a "Reveal"—a moment where the truth comes out. Any particular reveal is not necessarily the only truthful time nor does it reveal all of the truth. It is merely a moment of truth in a play.

1.  "… on the road sometimes I just want to grab you sometimes and just kiss the life outa you." Willy is falling into his own guilt, and his insecurity about his ability to sell—as well as his sheer loneliness—have hit him here in the fact of Linda's compassion and support.

2.  "There's so much I want to make for …" The scene has blended; two women are there, Linda and Willy's mistress. Things are getting jumbled and ugly.

3.  "You picked me, heh?" Willy is falling for flattery because, as he perversely teaches his boys, it is most important that a man "be liked."

4.  "Well, bottoms up!" Willy needs to feel sexy, needed, "manly" in the old-fashioned sense of the term. Where is Linda's place in his mind right now?

5.  Willy gives this strange woman stockings. These are stockings that Linda is entitled to—stockings that were meant for her. In this moment, Willy truly betrays his beloved wife. He gives what is rightfully hers to a stranger, in exchange for being liked, and getting sex.

6.  "I'll make it all up to you Linda …" Willy realizes that this is something that probably cannot be fixed, only hidden. Biff's discovery of the mistress in Act 2 becomes the catalyst for chaos.

7.  "I won't have you mending stockings in this house! Now throw them out!" The flashback of his cheating played out in real time while Linda fixes the dregs he's left her is an emotional incident that Willy cannot face. In the end, the threat that Biff might make him face up to Linda is a brutal and powerful moment.

8.  *"You'll give him the answers!"* Bernard is only telling Willy the truth: Biff is screwing up. Willy needs Biff to succeed because his son is his one hope for meaning and redemption.

9.  *"He's too rough with the girls, Willy. All the mothers are afraid of him!"* Linda escalates the speed of the crisis.

10. *"(The Woman's laugh is heard.)"* This is the laughter of consequence; from the stockings to Biff's failing grades, Willy's flaw, his desperate need to be liked, have led to a day where it all might unravel. And eventually it does.

11. *"You want him to be a worm like Bernard?"* Bernard, we learn in Act 2, is far from a worm as an adult. He's the actual success Willy insists he is raising his boys to be.

12. *"I never in my life told him anything but decent things."* Earlier, when Biff is caught with the stolen football, we saw graphic evidence of the falsehood here. Now we see that the falsehoods and the lies and the excuses have come to the point of consequence. Now the incident[s] that make the story flow with an inevitable rush to the climactic moment[s] has begun.

Rising action/plot complication is essential in moving along a story. Things, meaning events physical, emotional, and philosophical, need to gain momentum for the audience to remain engaged in the narrative. At this point, it becomes unwieldy for us to go line to line, since the actual events that Miller puts into the play from this point are classic story (or for another term, plot) elements, and they all raise the speed of the action. Here is a synopsis of what we see built up from the preceding flashback until the end of Act 1. Here are the events that raise the action and complicate the plot:

Willy continues to have many flashbacks, including scenes with his sinister and recently deceased brother, Ben, a brother who abandoned Willy as a child and went off to become fabulously rich, at least according to the cynical and malevolent man we meet as Ben in these moments. Willy gets into a nasty fight with his neighbor, Charley, who comes over during a late night outburst of rage by Willy and tries to calm him down by playing cards until Willy accuses him of cheating. During this card, game Charley offers Willy a job, which Willy turns down and, in fact, considers an insult. This is the start of the escalation.

Biff reveals that he has a plan to go see a former employer, a well-connected and successful businessman in Manhattan named Bill Oliver and ask him for a large loan to start his own business. He says he plans to do this tomorrow. In an angry discussion with his mother (Linda), Biff talks about how embarrassing Willy's outbursts and wandering off into past times during conversation have become. This causes Linda to let both Happy and Biff have it emotionally with two enormous revelations. The first is that Willy has lost his salary. He is now on 100 percent commission and therefore has to borrow $50 a week from Charley and pretend it is his salary because he doesn't know that Linda knows. This is a huge jump in action, since we find that Willy is not only mentally trapped in the past, he is facing an ignominious end to his career in the present. Willy drives off every day to buyers who consider him old, obsolete, and is actually not doing well selling his product. This is quite a reveal. Linda then drops an even more enormous bombshell on the boys. She lets them know that she suspects that his recent problems with traffic accidents are apparently not unintentional—they are suicide attempts. The boys disagree until Linda shows them a small rubber tube she has found in the basement attached to the gas pipe of the heater. This pipe can only be explained as a tube through which Willy can inhale a deadly dose of gas. She goes on to tell Biff and Happy that every day she finds it, and then every day she removes it. With this evidence, the boys cannot argue: their father is seeking death. Biff promises to do his best to become a respectable son by pursuing his business deal. Happy talks about doing his best to become a more respectable, ultimately married, man. Buoyed with this news, Willy declares that he is going to Manhattan himself tomorrow, to enter the office of his company, and demand they give him a non-traveling job with a salary. There are still a few flashbacks and a fight between Biff and Willy that gets very unkind because Willy keeps telling Linda to shut up, which incenses Biff. Biff gives Willy a veiled threat about revealing his road infidelity to Linda. Willy slinks off to bed, and Biff apologizes to him. As Act 1 closes, we see Linda and Willy in bed and Linda asks straight out what Biff is holding against Willy. Willy avoids the answer, and the act ends with this poetic and almost exotically foreshadowing sentence: "Gee, look at the moon moving between the buildings!"

So now the characters onstage and we, the audience, have a lot of action and complication occurring. Things are moving fast, and the next day, the "tomorrow" during which Biff will get his startup money and Willy will get his Manhattan job with a salary, is now a day that those in the theatre are dying to see. Because of how much the stakes have been raised by the reveals, the plot complications, and the rising action, we cannot wait to find out how the scenario ultimately unfolds. We are set up for Act 2, all of which takes place on that fateful "tomorrow" and during which we experience, as audience and actors, the climax/catharsis of the play. In an epilogue, which is too short to call it its own act, the denouement occurs to tie up as many loose ends as possible.

It is important to reiterate that in a story with this level of complexity, the cathartic/climactic moment will actually be a series of moments, but ultimately the format is Aristotlean as far as the storytelling elements of a "Well Made Play."

The climax in Aristotle's view was a specific moment, and very often in a play that can be true. However, in *Death of a Salesman*, there are several moments. In fact, the climax is contained in a very emotional scene, a scene in which most—but not all—of the truth comes out. It is a terrible confrontation after a disastrous day in New York City in which Biff not only doesn't get the loan, he doesn't even meet the man he was going to ask for it. Willy not only doesn't get the New York job, he gets fired entirely. Happy deserts Willy at the restaurant to pick up some women and goes as far as telling the women that Willy isn't his father, he's just "some guy." Rather than footnote this section as we did with the earlier passages, the author would like the reader to simply read it and take in the nuances and shifts and emotional bursts so we can comment afterward. (We will also do this with the denouement.) The climax/catharsis, the scene in which the entire narrative emotionally blows up, takes place back at the house:

> WILLY (*suddenly conscious of Biff, turns and looks up at him, then begins picking up the packages of seeds in confusion.*):

Where the hell is that seed? *(Indignantly.)* You can't see nothing out here! They boxed in the whole goddam neighborhood!

BIFF: There are people all around here. Don't you realize that?

WILLY: I'm busy. Don't bother me.

BIFF *(taking the hoe from Willy)*: I'm saying good-by to you, Pop.

*(Willy looks at him, silent, unable to move.)* I'm not coming back any more.

WILLY: You're not going to see Oliver tomorrow?

BIFF: I've got no appointment, Dad.

WILLY: He put his arm around you, and you've got no appointment?

BIFF: Pop, get this now, will you? Everytime I've left it's been a fight that sent me out of here. Today I realized something about myself and I tried to explain it to you and I—I think I'm just not smart enough to make any sense out of it for you.

To hell with whose fault it is or anything like that. *(He takes*

*Willy's arm.)* Let's just wrap it up, heh? Come on in, we'll tell

Mom. *(He gently tries to pull Willy to left.)*

WILLY *(frozen, immobile, with guilt in his voice)*: No, I don't want to see her.

BIFF: Come on! *(He pulls again, and Willy tries to pull away.)*

WILLY *(highly nervous)*: No, no, I don't want to see her.

BIFF *(tries to look into Willy's face, as if to find the answer there)*:

Why don't you want to see her?

WILLY *(more harshly now)*: Don't bother me, will you?

BIFF: What do you mean, you don't want to see her? You don't want them calling you yellow, do you? This isn't your fault; it's me, I'm a bum. Now come inside! *(Willy strains to get away.)*

Did you hear what I said to you?

*(Willy pulls away and quickly goes by himself into the house. Biff follows.)*

LINDA (to Willy): Did you plant, dear?

BIFF (at the door, to Linda). All right, we had it out. I'm going and I'm not writing any more.

LINDA (going to Willy in the kitchen): I think that's the best way, dear. 'Cause there's no use drawing it out, you'll just never get along.

(Willy doesn't respond.)

BIFF: People ask where I am and what I'm doing, you don't know, and you don't care. That way it'll be off your mind and you can start brightening up again. All right? That clears it, doesn't it? (Willy is silent, and Biff goes to him.) You gonna wish me luck, scout? (He extends his hand.) What do you say?

LINDA: Shake his hand, Willy.

WILLY (turning to her, seething with hurt): There's no necessity to mention the pen at all, y'know.

BIFF (gently): I've got no appointment, Dad.

WILLY (erupting fiercely). He put his arm around …?

BIFF: Dad, you're never going to see what I am, so what's the use of arguing? If I strike oil I'll send you a check. Meantime forget

I'm alive.

WILLY (to Linda): Spite, see?

BIFF: Shake hands, Dad.

WILLY: Not my hand.

BIFF: I was hoping not to go this way.

WILLY: Well, this is the way you're going. Good-by.

(Biff looks at him a moment, then turns sharply and goes to the stairs.)

WILLY (stops him with): May you rot in hell if you leave this house!

BIFF (turning): Exactly what is it that you want from me?

WILLY: I want you to know, on the train, in the mountains, in the valleys, wherever you go, that you cut down your life for spite!

BIFF: No, no.

WILLY: Spite, spite, is the word of your undoing! And when you're down and out, remember what did it. When you're rotting somewhere beside the railroad tracks, remember, and don't you dare blame it on me!

BIFF: I'm not blaming it on you!

WILLY: I won't take the rap for this, you hear?

*(Happy comes down the stairs and stands on the bottom step, watching.)*

BIFF: That's just what I'm telling you!

WILLY *(sinking into a chair at a table, with full accusation)*:

You're trying to put a knife in me—don't think I don't know what you're doing!

BIFF: All right, phony! Then let's lay it on the line. *(He whips the rubber tube out of his pocket and puts it on the table.)*

HAPPY: You crazy …

LINDA: Biff! *(She moves to grab the hose, but Biff holds it down with his hand.)*

BIFF: Leave it there! Don't move it!

WILLY *(not looking at it)*: What is that?

BIFF: You know goddam well what that is.

WILLY *(caged, wanting to escape)*: I never saw that.

BIFF: You saw it. The mice didn't bring it into the cellar! What is this supposed to do, make a hero out of you? This supposed to make me sorry for you?

WILLY: Never heard of it.

BIFF: There'll be no pity for you, you hear it? No pity!

WILLY *(to Linda)*: You hear the spite!

BIFF: No, you're going to hear the truth—what you are and what I am!

LINDA: Stop it!

WILLY: Spite!

HAPPY (*coming down toward Biff*): You cut it now!

BIFF (*to Happy*): The man don't know who we are! The man is gonna know! (*To Willy.*) We never told the truth for ten minutes in this house!

HAPPY: We always told the truth!

BIFF (*turning on him*): You big blow, are you the assistant buyer?

You're one of the two assistants to the assistant, aren't you?

HAPPY: Well, I'm practically—

BIFF: You're practically full of it! We all are! And I'm through with it. (*To Willy.*) Now hear this, Willy, this is me.

WILLY: I know you!

BIFF: You know why I had no address for three months? I stole a suit in Kansas City and I was in jail. (*To Linda, who is sobbing.*)

Stop crying. I'm through with it. (*Linda turns away from them, her hands covering her face.*)

WILLY: I suppose that's my fault!

BIFF: I stole myself out of every good job since high school!

WILLY: And whose fault is that?

BIFF: And I never got anywhere because you blew me so full of hot air I could never stand taking orders from anybody! That's whose fault it is!

WILLY: I hear that!

LINDA: Don't, Biff!

BIFF: It's goddam time you heard that! I had to be boss big shot in two weeks, and I'm through with it.

WILLY: Then hang yourself! For spite, hang yourself!

BIFF: No! Nobody's hanging himself, Willy! I ran down eleven flights with a pen in my hand today. And suddenly I stopped, you hear me? And in the middle of that office building, do you hear this? I stopped in the middle of that building and I saw—the sky. I saw the things that I love in this world. The work and the food and time to sit and smoke. And I looked at the pen and said to myself, what the hell am I grabbing this for? Why am I trying to become what I don't want to be? What am I doing in an office, making a contemptuous, begging fool of myself, when all I want is out there, waiting for me the minute I say I know who I am! Why can't I say that, Willy? *(He tries to make Willy face him, but Willy pulls away and moves to the left.)*

WILLY *(with hatred, threateningly)*: The door of your life is wide open!

BIFF: Pop! I'm a dime a dozen, and so are you!

WILLY *(turning on him now in an uncontrolled outburst)*: I am not a dime a dozen! I am Willy Loman, and you are Biff Loman!

*(Biff starts for Willy, but is blocked by Happy. In his fury, Biff seems on the verge of attacking his father.)*

BIFF: I am not a leader of men, Willy, and neither are you. You were never anything but a hard-working drummer who landed in the ash can like all the rest of them! I'm one dollar an hour, Willy I tried seven states and couldn't raise it. A buck an hour!

Do you gather my meaning? I'm not bringing home any prizes any more, and you're going to stop waiting for me to bring them home!

WILLY *(directly to Biff)*: You vengeful, spiteful mutt!

*(Biff breaks from Happy. Willy, in fright, starts up the stairs. Biff grabs him.)*

BIFF *(at the peak of his fury)*: Pop, I'm nothing! I'm nothing, Pop.

Can't you understand that? There's no spite in it any more.

I'm just what I am, that's all.

*(Biff's fury has spent itself, and he breaks down, sobbing, holding on to Willy, who dumbly fumbles for Biff's face.)*

WILLY *(astonished)*: What're you doing? What're you doing? *(To Linda.)* Why is he crying?

BIFF *(crying, broken)*: Will you let me go, for Christ's sake? Will you take that phony dream and burn it before something happens?

*(Struggling to contain himself, he pulls away and moves to the stairs.)* I'll go in the morning. Put him—put him to bed.

*(Exhausted, Biff moves up the stairs to his room.)*

WILLY *(after a long pause, astonished, elevated)*: Isn't that—isn't that remarkable? Biff—he likes me!

Arguably, the ultimate climax, the ultimate catharsis contained in the play takes place at the very end of this passage when Willy—poor, small, suicidal Willy—says, "Biff—he likes me!" It is utterly tragic but it is also the moment where Willy finally gets what he has wanted since things went wrong on the road and his beloved son caught him having an affair. Willy, who can only see things through the lens of monetary success or personal popularity, has not the *love* of his son as a comfort; he has the knowledge that his son *likes* him. Willy uses this comforting information to finally kill himself, seeing it as a way to give his wife and children a financial gift that will propel them to great things. In the end, Willy leaves and drives his car into the darkness and dies in an accident.

It is also important to point out that scene contains Biff's moment of climax/catharsis as well. He lets the family know that he's a thief. He lets Willy know that he is "a dime a dozen" and that he can live with that. Ultimately, he gives Willy the gift of completely writing him off, a gift Willy tragically misinterprets and uses as his trigger to die. A lot of emotion takes place in this segment, a lot of truth-telling (although whether the truth about Willy's affair[s] on the road are ever known by Linda, or if she actually knew anyway and just never let on) occurs. The characters onstage and the people in the seats are exhausted. It is time to wrap up. It is time for the audience move on, to go get coffee and talk with friends about the play. All that is left before that are a few loose ends, the denouement, which takes place in a scene that Miller calls "Requiem," and while it is contained in Act 2, it is really something after Act 2. There is a scene at the gravesite:

## requiem

CHARLEY: It's getting dark, Linda.

*(Linda doesn't react. She stares at the grave.)*

BIFF: How about it, Mom? Better get some rest, heh? They'll be closing the gate soon.

*(Linda makes no move. Pause.)*

HAPPY *(deeply angered)*: He had no right to do that. There was no necessity for it. We would've helped him.

CHARLEY (grunting): Hmmm.

BIFF: Come along, Mom.

LINDA: Why didn't anybody come?

CHARLEY: It was a very nice funeral.

LINDA: But where are all the people he knew? Maybe they blame him.

CHARLEY: Naa. It's a rough world, Linda. They wouldn't blame him.

LINDA: I can't understand it. At this time especially. First time in thirty-five years we were just about free and clear. He only needed a little salary. He was even finished with the dentist.

CHARLEY: No man only needs a little salary.

LINDA: I can't understand it.

BIFF: There were a lot of nice days. When he'd come home from a trip; or on Sundays, making the stoop; finishing the cellar; putting on the new porch; when he built the extra bathroom; and put up the garage. You know something, Charley, there's more of him in that front stoop than in all the sales he ever made.

CHARLEY: Yeah. He was a happy man with a batch of cement.

LINDA: He was so wonderful with his hands.

BIFF: He had the wrong dreams. All, all, wrong.

HAPPY (almost ready to fight Biff): Don't say that!

BIFF: He never knew who he was.

CHARLEY (stopping Happy's movement and reply. To Biff): Nobody dast blame this man. You don't understand: Willy was a salesman. And for a salesman, there is no rock bottom to the life. He don't put a bolt to a nut, he don't tell you the law or give you medicine. He's man way out there in the blue, riding on a smile and a Shoeshine. And when they start not smiling back—that's an earthquake. And then you get yourself a couple of spots on your hat, and you're finished. Nobody dast blame this man. A salesman is got to dream, boy. It comes with the territory.

BIFF: Charley, the man didn't know who he was.

HAPPY (infuriated): Don't say that!

BIFF: Why don't you come with me, Happy?

HAPPY: I'm not licked that easily. I'm staying right in this city, and I'm gonna beat this racket! *(He looks at Biff, his chin set.)*

The Loman Brothers!

BIFF: I know who I am, kid.

HAPPY: All right, boy. I'm gonna show you and everybody else that Willy Loman did not die in vain. He had a good dream. It's the only dream you can have—to come out number-one man.

He fought it out here, and this is where I'm gonna win it for him.

BIFF *(with a hopeless glance at Happy, bends toward his mother)*:

Let's go, Mom.

LINDA: I'll be with you in a minute. Go on, Charley. *(He hesitates.)*

I want to, just for a minute. I never had a chance to say good-by.

*(Charley moves away, followed by Happy. Biff remains a slight distance up and left of Linda. She sits there, summoning herself. The flute begins, not far away, playing behind her speech.)*

LINDA: Forgive me, dear. I can't cry. I don't know what it is, I can't cry. I don't understand it. Why did you ever do that? Help me Willy, I can't cry. It seems to me that you're just on another trip. I keep expecting you. Willy, dear, I can't cry. Why did you do it? I search and search and I search, and I can't understand it, Willy. I made the last payment on the house today. Today, dear. And there'll be nobody home. *(A sob rises in her throat.)*

We're free and clear. *(Sobbing more fully, released.)* We're free.

*(Biff comes slowly toward her.)* We're free … We're free … *(Biff lifts her to her feet and moves out up right with her in his arms.*

*Linda sobs quietly. Bernard and Charley come together and follow them, followed by Happy. Only the music of the flute is left on the darkening stage as over the house the hard towers of the apartment buildings rise into sharp focus, and the curtain falls.)*

Charley eulogizes Willy perfectly and honestly. Biff is moving on, leaving, hopefully to finally live the life he actually wants to live. Happy is defiant. He refuses to say his father's life was a failure and vows to live Willy's dream for him. Finally, we are left with Linda's gut-wrenching good-bye. At first she tells us she cannot cry; then it happens, and we, the audience, leave with her final words as a haunting coda to the entire play:

Linda: We're free … We're free …

It is important to reiterate that in a story with this level of complexity, the cathartic/climactic moment will actually be a series of moments, but ultimately the format is Aristotlean concerning the storytelling elements of a Well-Made Play."

So let's get back to how we use these elements in our everyday speech and storytelling. Suppose you go out to a party with friends. Again, suppose that you meet someone whom you find attractive and try to speak to that person but all night long you never get the chance because someone else monopolizes the attention of your unrequited affection. By the end of the party, you never get to talk with the object of your desire. The way you would tell that story to your friends the next day would most likely follow the format set down by Homer and Aristotle more than 2,000 years ago. For purposes of demonstration, let's make our protagonist a woman.

First you'd meet a friend for coffee and you'd say "I went to a party last night at Joey's apartment."

That's classic Exposition.

Then you'd say, "I saw this really good-looking guy there, and I was dying all night to strike up a conversation, but I couldn't get near him because my so-called friend Janice kept him talking all night."

That is classic introduction of conflict.

Then you would relate the inciting incident, which might be: "So Janice walks right up to me and Joey, and says to him, 'Could we talk privately for a minute?'"

Then comes the **Rising Action/Plot Complication**: "She walked off with him for **an hour**! I stood there looking foolish in front of everybody for all of that time, and of course Tiffany has to come up and tell me that they've been hanging around a lot in the dorm."

Then you'd bring the story to a head by saying, "So, when she came back, I walked up to her and screamed 'I hate you!' and dumped a glass of cranberry juice on her head. Then I told Joey he wasn't worth my time and I left." This would be the climax/catharsis.

Finally, you'd say, "Then I got asked to leave the party, so I went to the diner and ate pie until the sun came up." That is **Denouement**.

The last part of your anecdote would be, "So I don't think I'm going back to Joey's anytime soon."

And that is the **Resolution/End** of the story.

So you see the Elements of Aristotle and the aspects of storytelling that were set down by not only Homer but his historic predecessors are in no way beyond the understanding of a casual theatregoer in the 21st century; you do indeed know them by heart and use them each and every day of your life.

a play, and how it is performed, can fall into various styles and genres. For instance, a musical is likely to be presented to an audience in a much different way than a nonmusical dramatic piece. How the show is conveyed to the audience with regard to its presentation generally falls into two main approaches: PRESENTATIONAL and REPRESENTATIONAL theatre.

However, before we can make the distinction between those terms, we need to define a concept in theatre which is known as *THE FOURTH WALL*. If you attend a play staged on a very realistic set, let us say a living room in New York City (like the one where Oscar lives in Neil Simon's *The Odd Couple*), you take your seat, and when the curtain comes up you see a messy and somewhat small apartment. There will be tables and chairs and lamps and maybe a kitchenette. Very real-looking windows with buildings of the Manhattan Skyline showing outside of them will be in the living area. The apartment will look like a place where a real person is living a real life. That is, except for one small difference. The apartment will only have three walls at most. There will not be a fourth wall for a rather obvious reason. We, the audience, need a way to see in; we

# 13: style

need the actors and action to be visually accessible. A realistic fourth wall would block this action from our sight, so it isn't there.

Or is it? The 4th wall in many plays still exists, but it is entirely imaginary. It is a conceptual wall that separates the players from the witnesses to the play. An actor can, in fact, do something (and often does in many plays) called *BREAKING THE 4TH WALL* by stepping out of the physical or conceptual boundaries of the set and addressing the audience.

How the fourth wall is dealt with is at the heart of the distinction between a presentational and a representational performance of a play. PRESENTATIONAL/ REPRESENTATIONAL: The terms are fairly simple to define, but besides the fourth wall concept, we need to set the table just a little bit more before we define them. We must revisit the event that is a performance of a play.

This is a play: Actors come out on stage and portray the story and the lines of the script while an audience watches. Generally, this is the experience of theatre. The play may be extremely symbolic; extremely real; absurd; funny; sad; both funny AND sad; wordless; or any one of an almost infinite panoply of methods or styles through which the playwright, director, and actors want to tell the story or make their message heard. The question of whether

*Noël Coward (December 16, 1899–March 26, 1973) was an English playwright, composer, director, actor, and singer known for his wit and flamboyance.*

a production of a play is presentational or representational comes down to this intrinsic question: Does the performance acknowledge the presence of the audience (and let the audience know that they are acknowledging them) or not? Do the actors speak directly or present directly to those who watch, or do they ignore them in an attempt to give the illusion to those who watch that they are seeing a real event occur and that they are looking into it without the characters knowing they are being watched? How far does the production go to respect, acknowledge, or break the fourth wall?

A **presentational** performance acknowledges the audience. It makes no pretentions that there aren't seats with (hopefully) paid audience members watching. In presentational theatre, entire monologues may be spoken directly to the audience. The audience may even be asked to respond or come onto the stage with the actors during certain segments of the play. There is no barrier; the show is there and lets you know that you see those who are performing it and that they see you. As a general rule, you will find that most musicals are done in a style that is largely presentational, but many plays, even extremely emotionally intense dramas, also are produced presentationally.

**Representational** theatre does not acknowledge the audience. In the representational approach, the audience is assumed to be looking into the world of the play without the knowledge of the characters in the story. The actors are trying to create a pure illusion of reality. *This is all really happening and you are peeking into the private world of the characters without their cognition of your observation.* Certain plays simply demand this convention. They demand that the story be seen by an audience without the characters' awareness of being seen. Dramatic pieces come immediately to mind, but many comedies could be ruined if the fourth wall was broken. The director and actors and all of the creative team need to know whether their play is best served by taking either a presentational or representational approach.

An easy way to remember the difference is this: "Presentational" contains the word "present." We, the actors, are giving you a present and acknowledging that you have received it. We want to watch you open that present and give credence to your reaction to it.

"Representational" starts with the word "represent." In this case, we, the actors, are trying to represent reality. We are still giving you the gift of a performance, but if we let you know we watched you open that gift, we spoil the illusion of pure reality.

As always, there are instances in which a play works within both strictures. Many plays contain lines or entire scenes that are **asides**. An aside is when a character briefly, within a scene, talks directly to the audience instead of their fellow characters onstage. Here's a nice example from *Richard III* by William Shakespeare, slightly edited. To set the scenario, the reader needs to know that Richard, who is speaking here, doesn't mean anything he's saying to the people he is addressing. He despises almost all of them and by the end of the play kills most of them. However, in the presence of the king (Richard is not yet king at this point of the play), he puts on a masterful display of false oratory:

*Garrick as the title character in Shakespeare's* Richard III

RICHARD: (Addressing the Court of the King)

'Tis death to me to be at enmity;

I hate it, and desire all good men's love.

First, madam, I entreat true peace of you,

Which I will purchase with my duteous service;—

Of you, my noble cousin Buckingham,

If ever any grudge were lodged between us, or of you,

Dukes, earls, lords, gentlemen; indeed, of all.

I do not know that Englishman alive

With whom my soul is any jot at odds

More than the infant that is born tonight.

I thank my God for my humility.

"I thank my God for my humility" is something said aloud not for the other characters present in the scene, it is a line spoken directly to the audience for ironic effect. Presented to the audience well, this line actually pulls a belly laugh. Richard is not at all humble and he knows it. He knows that the others in the court know it. The speech, up to the aside, is entirely disingenuous, so Shakespeare has Richard speak right to the people in the seats and acknowledge it. Other than the aside, which obviously is a presentational moment, the rest of the scene is presented as a real discourse between the characters of the court. It is representational during those moments.

Shakespeare also provides us with another type of theatrical moment that skirts the presentational/ representational line. This is the convention known as a **soliloquy**. A soliloquy is a moment, perhaps an entire speech, in which a character says aloud what she or he is thinking for the benefit of the audience so they know where the character's mind is going and what dilemmas it is facing in thought. In his comedy *Twelfth Night*, a comedy that gets great audience reaction to this day, Shakespeare creates a female character named Viola, who for many reasons is disguised as a man until the end of the story. Viola is in love with a man, and the woman that man is in love with, Olivia, has fallen in love with Viola as a man. Viola, realizing how complicated her life has become and realizing what a challenge she faces, gives this speech aloud, this **soliloquy**, in which the audience learns her thoughts. Although Viola speaks this entire speech aloud, she does not acknowledge those of us who watch:

> VIOLA: I left no ring with her. What means this lady?
>
> Fortune forbid my outside have not charmed her.
>
> She made good view of me; indeed, so much
>
> That, as methought, her eyes had lost her tongue,
>
> For she did speak in starts distractedly.
>
> She loves me sure; the cunning of her passion
>
> Invites me in this churlish messenger.
>
> None of my lord's ring? Why, he sent her none.
>
> I am the man. If it be so, as 'tis,
>
> Poor lady, she were better love a dream.
>
> Disguise, I see thou art a wickedness
>
> Wherein the pregnant enemy does much.
>
> How easy is it for the proper false

In women's waxen hearts to set their forms!

Alas, our frailty is the cause, not we,

For such as we are made of, such we be.

How will this fadge? My master loves her dearly;

And I (poor monster) fond as much on him;

And she (mistaken) seems to dote on me.

What will become of this? As I am man,

My state is desperate for my master's love.

As I am woman (now alas the day!),

What thriftless sighs shall poor Olivia breathe?

O Time, thou must untangle this, not I;

It is too hard a knot for me t' untie.

A speech like this is concurrently presentational and representational. Even to the present day, Shakespeare is certainly not the only playwright to use the concepts of asides and soliloquies to guide the audience along the narrative of a play.

†he term 'Genre' is so common in daily usage that it may seem unnecessary to explain. However, to truly understand not just how theatre is created and performed but also how it is promoted, genre is necessary to define. "Promotion" of art can be a bit of a dirty word because to some it implies that the primary intent of a production is to make a profit from its creation for the artists and whoever may have invested in it. It means, to some, that the pure core of the piece created has been commercialized, or even worse, turned into just another product in the marketplace. This argument has validity on both sides: At its best, art is truthful and uncorrupted by financial considerations. On the other hand, there *is indeed a marketplace in the arts, especially in entertainment*. We live in a consumer society and that means we have, on any given night when looking for entertainment, many options. This is now a world where a movie can be watched on a telephone. Since theatre doesn't really exist without an audience, *there must be people in the seats watching for it to exist as an art*. To get those people into those seats, therefore, the play must be promoted. If you ask any actor on the planet, they will tell you that it is easier to do a show for 5,000 people than five. That audience energy matters and

# 14: genre

often makes or breaks the quality of a given performance.

So, in theatre, what is genre and what is its relationship to promotion as well as the artistic value of a play?

Genre, generally, falls into two categories: comedy and drama. The familiar symbols for theatre, the sad and happy masks next to each other, represent this. But we all are aware that comedy and drama are not where describing a play ends. Even the most thematically light comedies, plays that simply are out to "get the laugh," usually have some dramatic moments. This is because it becomes hard for an audience to keep laughing at a character if they have absolutely no emotional investment in that character.

Therefore, the hero of the comedy is usually given a struggle, some pain, and adversity that she or he must overcome. Conversely, even the most tragic drama will as a general rule contain some comedy. A character, even one that dies in an utterly tragic manner by the end of the play, will often lose our empathy as audience members if they display no humor at any time. Culturally, especially in America, we tend to admire the protagonist who can "laugh in the face of disaster" or at least laugh at some time before the disaster. A critic will often refer to a drama that has no humor whatsoever as a melodrama. This

*Java Theatre Bird Mask*

is usually not a compliment given to the playwright by the reviewer. There is even a very common phrase used not only in theatre but in many aspects of our life that addresses this: "Comic Relief. " When it comes to theatrical drama, the word "relief" is absolutely poignant. To live with the pain of Hamlet's death, Ophelia's death, Polonius's death, Laertes' death, Gertrude's death, and even the death of Claudius, we need the relief of the humor that is provided by characters such as the gravediggers. Otherwise, the sheer weight of disaster within the story might become unreal or cartoonish. This is not to say that an effective and moving drama cannot be written without comic relief or that an effective comedy cannot be written without any drama.

Again, we must remember that we are talking about theatre, and that theatre is art. There are no unbreakable rules; there is only what occurs in the majority of instances. If the reader of this text decides to write a play with no comic relief whatsoever, and that play is simply the single most moving and meaningful dramatic work ever put on the page and then given life upon a stage, it will still be a beautiful work of art. It will also be special because it is the exception to the rule.

Genre, therefore, tends to include many hybrids containing various amounts of both comedy and drama. A mystery is likely to have some drop-dead funny moments. A farce is likely to have moments of tenderness or even deep meaning. As a culture, we have even have coined new terms such as dramedy and tragicomedy to address these kinds of shows.

So why even bother talking about genre? Once again, there is the issue of reaching your audience. The title of a play is very important. More often than not it tells us what kind of story we are going to see dramatized. However, the title might not be enough to get the general public interested in seeing the show. It might not let the people on the street know anything about the show whatsoever. (*August, Osage County* is a tremendous and award-winning piece of dark comedy written by Tracy Letts, but that title is merely a description of a time and place. The reader of this book only knows it is a dark comedy because the author described it that way within this parenthetical statement.) In promotion, you will quite frequently see a play described in such terms as, "The Best New Dramatic Comedy of the Year" or "A Riveting Evening of Mystery and Suspense." Genre not only helps the playwright keep track of the tone she or he desires in their work, it lets the potential ticket purchaser know what they are choosing to see. Even in a relatively small city, there are dozens of entertainment options on a given day available to the consumer. As mentioned before, they might not even involve getting out of bed if you have a phone within reach. To get the modern audience on their feet, out of the house, and into the theatre, we are going to need some enticement. That mass of humanity huddled under their blankets wants to know what they are buying tickets to see. Genre allows the promotional team of the theatrical company to quickly inform their patrons what the play is about.

When an actor begins to train, she will hear about the concept of being a "Triple Threat." This is a description of a performer who is proficient at acting, singing, and dance. Being gifted and trained at all three of these skills is coveted because it means an artist is versatile. More importantly, it is desirable to be a triple threat because in any given theatre season, a great many of the productions created all over the world are **Musicals**. Statistically, most Broadway seasons recently have been populated by a majority of shows that were, if not full musicals, at least shows that featured dance or songs. In some production years, this percentage has approached 80 percent of the available work for theatre artists. In short, a musical is big business and a big opportunity for artists; thus it is a form, along with acting in Shakespearean productions, that a potential stage actor must be willing to work in if he desires to be competitive in the business and make a living.

So where did **Musical Theatre** come from? Its roots are quite diverse and of course, go back at least as far as the Greeks, if not further. The use of song in worship and the use of theatrical storytelling in religious ritual were prevalent,

# 15: musical theatre

as we have said before, during the ancient Egyptian empire. It is well known that many parts of the classic Greek drama, including the work of the chorus, were sung and acted at the same time. Songs were often the focal point in medieval drama as well; in fact, many medieval dramas were essentially liturgical pageants. These ritual dramas, often sung in Latin, existed so as to recruit and reaffirm the Christian faith in a populace that still had strong pagan roots. During the Renaissance, Europe saw the ascendance of opera, especially in Italy. Opera, while not falling exactly under the aegis and definition of musical theatre, was nonetheless the acting and portrayal of stories through song. Opera remains a vital art form, and shares a great many aspects with what we call musical theatre today. The main difference between the genres lies in several areas, not the least of which is sheer scale. The magnificent operas of the Renaissance (and right up to the present day) depend a great deal on the concept of spectacle—huge sets, lavish costumes, and momentous music are elements of the opera that not all musicals share. It is also true, of course, that there are smaller-scale operas now (and have been in the past), but the grand artistic tours de force that were opera in the 16th century remain the predominant style of presenting the form today. Opera also differs from musical theatre (again with the caveat that sometimes these rules are bent and broken) in that it does not usually include spoken scenes and lines. Typically, in opera, the entire story presented to the audience is given in song. There are very few operas

*2008 Buffalo State production of* Hair

(and purists would argue that these aren't *true* operas) that have nonmusical speech in them.

Musical theatre's evolution toward the modern form began to move forward rapidly during the 1800s with the advent in several countries of theatrical entertainments that were presented in revue style. Burlesque and traveling variety shows in the United States began to coalesce into a form that, by the late 1800s, was known as vaudeville. Vaudeville shows included short melodramatic plays, monologists (the precursors of modern stand-up comics), magic acts, jugglers, and animal acts, but most especially, vaudeville relied a great deal upon music and singing. Popular music, from the songs of Stephen Foster ("Oh! Susanna," "Swanee," "I Dream Of Jeanie") to the early-20th-century works of Irving Berlin ("Blue Skies," "Alexander's Ragtime Band," "Let's Face the Music and Dance"), began to rise in popularity. American families would buy the sheet music for songs that gained a following in vaudeville to play and sing along with at home. In England, a very similar form of variety-based entertainment was exploding in popularity as well, and there it was known as the Music Hall. France had its cabarets, as well as the more risqué presentations found at the Moulin Rouge and the Folies Bergère, and Germany too saw a rapid growth of musical entertainment entwined with comedic sketches and short plays.

In New York, all of these influences from all of these nations were percolating as the entertainment dollar was heavily competed for by theatre owners and producers. Full-length musicals were inevitable when one looks back on the cultural factors in play at the time. Music, dance, and comedy were king, which explains—even during an era that was largely sexually repressed—the popularity of burlesque, an entertainment form that drew patrons even among the female population. The consensus among scholars is that the first "true" full-length musical was *The Black Crook*, which opened at a theatre known as Niblo's Garden in 1866 in New York City. (Niblo's Garden, while located on the avenue known as Broadway, was far from the modern Broadway Theatre District, closer to Greenwich Village than Times Square.) *The Black Crook* had a "Book" or "Libretto" (both of which are terms that describe a written script of scenes or a general scenario that functioned as the storytelling arc of the play), as well as songs that were written and given lyrics for the purpose of telling the story. Meanwhile, back in England, as the 1800s came to a close, there was a rapid growth in the popularity of Comic Operettas. These were full-length musicals with spoken dialogue that were known for clever humor and songs with rapidly presented lyrics that came to be called Patter Songs. The most enduring of these British shows were written by the team of Gilbert and Sullivan; their hilarious, madcap approach to storytelling would influence many vaudeville and musical theatre performers, including the Marx Brothers. Gilbert and Sullivan shows remain very popular. Frequent revivals of their works are presented all over, from Broadway to Bangkok and by specific Gilbert and Sullivan Societies worldwide. Examples of the genius of Gilbert and Sullivan include *The Pirates of Penzance*, *H.M.S. Pinafore*, and *The Mikado*.

As the 20th century dawned and Broadway became the nexus of the theatrical arts worldwide, musicals began to dominate. Talents such as George M. Cohan, who wrote dialogue, melodies, and lyrics for many enormous hit shows like *Little Johnny Jones*, were creating a world of musical storytelling. This musical storytelling, along with the continuing influence of the vaudeville variety revues, made stars of popular music composers like Irving Berlin and Jerome Kern. The dominance of Cohan, who not only wrote the material but was often the principal actor/dancer/singer in his shows, was based on a formula that demanded musical theatre to have well-defined heroes and villains, thwarted lovers, and themes of good versus evil. The formula demanded that by the end of the show the hero would triumph, the lovers would be united, and the villains and their evil machinations would be defeated and receive their public comeuppance. These early-20th-century American musicals were not necessarily works of

*2009 Buffalo State production of* Anything Goes

tremendous literary value, but they have left America with a legacy of uplifting, optimistic, and unapologetically patriotic songs such as "Grand Old Flag," "Yankee Doodle Dandy," and "Over There." After World War One, an artistic shift began to take place in musical theatre. Serious themes such as racial inequality, political strife, and the deeper reaches of the human psyche began to find a place in the shows being written and produced. The subject of race—perhaps one of the greatest unspoken taboos of the time—was especially laid open. It is important to note that the prevalence of **Minstrel Shows**, revues in which white performers performed in blackface makeup and used largely derogatory stereotypes of the African American population, had been and were still extremely popular since before the Civil War.

The very first film with a soundtrack, the first "**Talkie**," was Al Jolson's *The Jazz Singer*. This technical and creative milestone featured scenes that a modern audience would be embarrassed by, scenes in which Jolson, wearing blackface and using ethnic tropes, sang songs with exaggerated parodies of African American dialect and accent. Musicals such as *Show Boat*, which featured the heartbreakingly beautiful composition "Old Man River," a show-stopping number that lamented the plight of black slaves and included lyrics of great poignancy, such as this following stanza:

"You don't look up, you don't look down.

You don't dare make the rich boss frown.

Bend your knees and bow your head

And tote that barge until you're dead."

A song such as this, with lyrics as powerful as "tote that barge until you're dead," was not a lighthearted romp in the Cohan tradition, but rather a clarion call for the audience to acknowledge genuine inequities that existed not only in the **Antebellum** era but in the present as well. Musical theatre was beginning to grow up. Political satire such as that found in 1932's Pulitzer Prize–winning *Of Thee I Sing* by George and Ira Gershwin, Morrie Ryskind, and the preeminent Algonquin Round Table humorist George S. Kaufman, became the set pieces that would carry musical theatre in America through both the Great Depression and World War Two. **A Golden Era** was coming, with legends such as Jerome Kern, Rodgers and Hart, and finally, the transcendent

*2012 Buffalo State production of* Dames at Sea

Rodgers and Hammerstein creating important works of art—musicals with often quite serious messages and themes such as racism, sexual inequality and violence, and the after-effects of war. Even seemingly benign works like *Oklahoma* looked past the jingoism of Cohan and the early plays of the 1900s and explored the darker corners of the human psyche. Rodgers and Hammerstein shattered the tropes of safety and demanded thought from their audiences with creations such as *Carousel*, *The King and I*, and *South Pacific*. The music often was light and airy, the dancing was energetic and engaging, but the troubles of the real world were not ignored in these shows. This musical maturity was furthered by the writer/composer/dramatist Stephen Sondheim, arguably the greatest artist of the musical theatre form.

As a boy of ten, Sondheim found himself as a playmate of James Hammerstein, whose father, Oscar Hammerstein II, became both an artistic mentor and a father figure. Writing and composing became Sondheim's raison d'être and he burst into international prominence when he wrote the lyrics to accompany Leonard Bernstein's music in *West Side Story*. This breakthrough work was an adaptation of Shakespeare's *Romeo and Juliet* with a book by Arthur Laurents. *West Side Story* became an international sensation, not only on stage but in film. *A Funny Thing Happened on the Way to the Forum*, a tremendously successful comedy based on the works of the ancient Roman playwright, Plautus, opened on Broadway in 1963 and won several Tony Awards, further establishing Sondheim as a major creative star. As Sondheim's voice—both as the writer of dialogue and composer of music—developed, his work began to if not dominate, then substantially influence, the tone of musical theatre. Experiments with form such as *Company*, explorations of extremely dark (to the point of macabre) comedy in operatic fashion such as *Sweeney Todd*, fantastic and Impressionism-inspired works such as *Sunday in the Park with George* and *Into the Woods* have made Stephen Sondheim (with significant credit due to several collaborators with which he worked, such as Hal Prince, John Weidman, and James Lapine) simply a legend in the musical theatre oeuvre. Sondheim's trademark will always be the sophistication of his lyrics and his occasionally cynical and often unsentimental view of relationships, a depth epitomized in the mournful but lovely lyrics of songs like "Send in the Clowns."

During the 1960s and 1970s, however, Sondheim wasn't the only thing happening in musical theatre. The societal upheaval of the Vietnam War era and the immense popularity of rock and roll music converged on Broadway to become a genre known as "Rock Opera" or "Rock Musical." The breakthrough of this form was the seminal musical *Hair*. This rock musical was a celebration of the Flower Power movement along with sending a strong antiwar message. It became a huge hit on Broadway and spun off several Top 40 hits on the radio. Religious-themed works with rock music as their backbone, such as *Jesus Christ Superstar* and *Godspell*, were also major successes. As the 1970s melted into the 1980s, Andrew Lloyd Webber and Tim

Rice created many shows with tremendously successful runs. The aforementioned *Jesus Christ Superstar*, *Joseph and the Amazing Technicolor Dreamcoat*, and *Evita* were all major hits in both the West End of London and on Broadway. Webber went on to use the poetry of T. S. Eliot to create *Cats* and also gave the world *The Phantom of the Opera*. Webber's work remains in constant production to this day.

As the 21$^{st}$ century moves along, the musical has seen the ascendance of the jukebox musical, theatrical revues and full musical stories that primarily use existing popular songs and often are homages to musical legends like Elvis, Buddy Holly, the Beatles, and the evolution of music itself. Starting with the smash revue *Beatlemania* in the late 1970s right up to *Mamma Mia*, a juggernaut based on the songs of ABBA (as of this book's writing, *Mamma Mia* is still enjoying successful stage productions worldwide), the jukebox musical has become a staple of the musical theatre. While these shows seem to be the harbinger of a particularly kitschy era in stage musical history, the immense popularity and critical and financial success of powerful, challenging, and even downright profane works such as the scathingly satirical political comedy *The Book of Mormon* promise that musical theatre will always evolve—as nonmusical theatre has through the centuries—and reflect the society that contains it.

† he authors believe that after discussing musical theatre from its historical perspective, it is important to speak about dance, not so much as a historical overview, but as it is learned and presented by dancers and choreographers. Dance is, indeed, its own discipline, and there are many wonderful troupes worldwide that present styles as diverse as the ballet and hip hop. These dance concerts, while related to theatre in many ways, stand as their own art form separate from theatre. They are the subject of thousands of books and entire fields of study. We decided to talk to choreographers with serious experience in both dance and theatre in order to give an overview of where the forms intersect. Here is what we learned:

# 16: the theatre of dance

# carlos jones, choreographer interview

*WHAT IS YOUR TRAINING/EXPERTISE? WHEN DID DANCING AND BEING A CHOREOGRAPHER BECOME A CAREER OPTION IN YOUR MIND?*

I was an undergrad at University of Missouri/KC Conservatory. My major was dance. I went to graduate school on a music scholarship. I started out to be a musician and became a choreographer. Theatre was frankly more of a secondary influence. I moved to LA [and] was able to get work in regional theatre. I did tours. I appeared as Cookie Monster in *Sesame Street Live* and that was my first Equity [the stage actors' union in the United States, Actors' Equity or AEA] gig. It was a great experience. Learning how to work with a mask was wonderful training for musical theatre format. I went back to school at UC Irvine for an MFA in Dance/American Vernacular (Tap Dance and Jazz) and a concentration in Theatre. Personally I was lucky that the junior high school and high school I went to had a very good arts program. It included drama as well as musical theatre. It really shaped my decision to go into theatre and dance as a career. It is important to teach young people the arts.

*FROM A CHOREOGRAPHER'S PERSPECTIVE, WHAT INFORMATION DO YOU THINK AN "INTRO TO THEATRE" TEXTBOOK ABSOLUTELY MUST CONTAIN?*

It is very important to show where choreography fits into theatre in nonmusical as well as musical theatre. It is important to stress that movement and dance are contained in every aspect of creating a show, whether there are songs in the play or not. Performers need to know how to use movement to create characters as well as speech and interpretation of texts. The students should know that there is a "wash" of Period Styles and history that influence dance and theatrical movement. They should be taught that these historical genres exist and have different aesthetics. In brief [from the point of view of dance and movement], they should understand how and why Shakespeare must be looked at differently than American Realism when you are creating theatre.

*DESCRIBE WHY THEATRE REMAINS A RELEVANT ART FORM IN THE 21$^{ST}$ CENTURY?*

Theatre presents an avenue for people to be able to explore human qualities. It gives people the opportunity to see different perspectives that are not of their world. Theatre, if it works, makes people think, coming away from their world for a bit and looking into the minds and points of view of total strangers.

*WHAT WOULD YOU SAY ARE THE "INTERSECTIONS" ARTISTICALLY BETWEEN DANCE AND THEATRE FOR PERFORMERS?*

As performers, whether dancers or actors, you always have the 5 W's [who, what, when, where, and why?]. Your character has to understand these questions regarding the roles you are playing. In both of theatre and dance the performer has to establish and answer the basic questions and

*2012 Buffalo State Dance Concert* Alternative Dimensions: A Multi-Sensory Experience

challenges their character faces and convey that to the audience. Mastery of your body and mind are important in both theatre and dance. When it comes down to it, whether it is in a dance concert or a straight dramatic play, Movement is Movement. If you understand what your body is doing and saying. If you have a trained and tuned instrument [performers refer to their body and voice as their instrument] and are capable of being in the moment, you will be effective as a dancer, an actor, or both. Being real, being "in character," has to be the same for both an actor and a dancer.

*HOW DO THEATRE AND DANCE DIVERGE?*

Mainly they diverge in how Time is perceived. I can say a sentence to you, such as "I love you," and you know the impact and meaning immediately. The same idea [saying "I love you"] may take thirty seconds in dance without words. In dance the moment has to be maintained longer to allow the audience to get the message.

*IN THEATRE, WHEN WE DISCUSS ACTING, WE TALK ABOUT CREATING A CHARACTER. HOW DO YOU APPROACH THE DEVELOPMENT OF A SPECIFIC CHARACTER IN DANCE? WHAT IS YOUR APPROACH TO CREATING THE EMOTIONAL LIFE OF YOUR DANCERS BEHIND THE CHOREOGRAPHY?*

Personally, I use imagery to create a place or something specific in their mind. I try to help guide the audience emotionally. To be specific, someone I am choreographing may be dancing the role of Blanche in an adaptation of *A Streetcar Named Desire* by Tennessee Williams. I'd begin the process by asking that dancer to imagine how an aging Southern belle like Blanche DuBois would move. Otherwise we look at character qualities: If you are a lost soul how would you look and stand? When you are lost emotionally how would you move? You look for the qualities that are the emotion behind the dance. If the dance concert is solo you don't necessarily talk about a character with a name, you talk about the emotions you want to convey. Often I will talk about what the dancer might remember about a specific event such as standing in a large field with the sun on her skin. How did she feel at that time? What was the joy like? The dancer then has to put

*Buffalo State College Spring Dance Recital* The Myth of MIles.

into her mind into that specific place during each performance and interpret it externally for the audience.

*HOW IMPORTANT DO YOU THINK IT IS FOR DANCE TO HAVE A MESSAGE, EITHER ARTISTICALLY, POLITICALLY, SPIRITUALLY, OR INTELLECTUALLY?*

It is not important to have a message, per se, but you must have a point of view. You can have the movement be the message; such as how do the leaves move in a Kansas field on a summer evening? How do we see the leaves leap in the wind? You can enjoy the aesthetics and esoterics of a piece, without necessarily engaging in the story's moral politics. I just want my choreography to contain good interesting movement that moves an audience emotionally.

*IS IT EASIER TO TEACH A DANCER TO ACT OR AN ACTOR TO DANCE?*

For me it is easier to teach an actor to dance. In my experience actors are more interested in learning how to move than dancers are learning how to speak. Dancers sometimes are terrified of verbal expression, although they express great emotion with their bodies. Much of this is because actors have to do physical comedy and period work—movement. Actors are asked to move more frequently than dancers are asked to speak.

*WHAT WOULD YOU CONSIDER THE ESSENTIAL CHOREOGRAPHER'S TOOLBOX?*

You have to essentially know time measurement [how to measure the length of dance pieces in musical time signatures] and how to establish theatrical beats, individual emotional moments within your work, within the structure of musical time signatures. A choreographer has to understand space and know how to use not only the space that the performers occupy but the actual theatre space that is being used. A choreographer has to understand Performance Energy, how a dancer enters a space and how they leave it. To sum it up a choreographer has to master and understand how the actors relate to one another and the space they share. A choreographer has to be able to collaborate with other artists such as directors and playwrights. If she/he is responsible for the dance elements of a stage musical the choreographer must work within the needs and concepts of the production. Simply stated, the choreography has to be in synch with the rest of the show.

# JOY GUARINO INTERVIEW

Multiple approaches to the same aspects of performance are a vital way for artists to become competitive in the world of theatre. As previously noted, one of the most coveted things an actor can be called is a triple threat: someone who can act, sing, and dance exceptionally. In this book, we are looking at the approaches taken by two different dance professionals when they instruct students. Dancer/choreographer Joy Guarino was kind enough to give us her input. Joy Guarino is an Assistant Professor of Dance at Buffalo State teaching a variety of studio technique clases, dance history, dance education, and choreography. She has developed courses, conducted research, and presented internationally on kinesthetic learning, dance/movement integration, and youth development. Currently, she and her students are involved in a cultural, artistic exchange with a dance faculty and students at Capital Normal University in Beijing. As a practitioner and consultant in the arts-in-education profession, she is committed to finding creative and practical ways of designing and implementing meaningful children's arts programs. Here's what she had to say.

*FIRST OF ALL, HOW DOES A TEACHER "TRAIN" A DANCER?*

Traditionally, in the department I've worked in for the last several years, we would begin by teaching a section called "Dance Appreciation." It was taught largely as a history course, discussing the careers and accomplishments of venerable dancer/choreographers like Martha Graham or Alvin Ailey as well as talking about the evolution of dance as an art form throughout the history of mankind. Personally I preferred to teach dance with more of a "hands-on" approach, letting the students find their own inner connection of what dance means to them. Not that we totally avoid history, it is just that now we teach our introductory students more of an aesthetics class. Learning the meaning and application of aesthetics is used so they see how dance can touch them personally. How they can experience the craft in a creative and emotional way.

*SO WHAT EXACTLY DO YOU MEAN WHEN YOU USE THE TERM "AESTHETICS?"*

Aesthetics in dance is formally defined as the Philosophy of Beauty. But to get away from the academic term and put it into words that mean something to the average person on the street, I'd describe an Aesthetic Experience as an event like seeing a sunset; witnessing something beautiful and emotionally moving. Describing those feelings that well up when you see a sunset are where words simply will not work. Words will not be able to let someone else know how a sunset's beauty moves you. It is something more profound inside. In class I'm very careful not to connect it to any specific philosophy or religion, but I describe aesthetics [in dance] as the individual seeing beauty or even negative experience as something spiritual; something which is simply better described nonverbally. In order to approach that spiritual (for lack of a better term) experience I have the dancers do a presentation. They come to the front and share with the class where they personally find that creative place that connects with their nonverbal spiritual self. Their aesthetic outlet could be many things like baking, gardening, or sewing. I have them present this outlet of their inner expression in front of their peers with an image, perhaps using PowerPoint or a drawing, anything visual; not verbal. This helps them connect to their aesthetic while also discovering what it is like to stand in front of an audience and deal with the pressure that comes from that experience. The point is found in connecting ***their*** aesthetic to ***us***. They can only really do that by connecting "inside out" with their art. I also teach flow, looking to be in the zone like an athlete: fully committing and letting the preparation and passion take over.

There are a lot of important aspects to what I teach and the core precepts break down in this way:

1. Dance Education. (Actual technique that a dancer must know to effectively use his or her body.)

2. Dance in Education/Dance as a Kinesthetic Art. This involves the use of movement to teach any idea; whether we are talking about an idea that is purely aesthetic, political, entertaining, or imparting new knowledge to those who watch the dance.

3. I stress, especially to my dancers who desire to work professionally, the **Art. *I want them to develop an aesthetic appreciation of dance and what it means to be a dancer/ choreographer*. To facilitate this I have to help them to be a better observer of dance. Sometimes the serious dancers are too concerned with body position as opposed to the feeling they are expressing. They become caught in worrying about things like "How high is my leg on this extension?" instead of concentrating on communicating the meaning of their movement to the audience.

4. I stress the need for them to respect their instrument, and that instrument of course is their body. A dancer has to be healthy and in shape and they cannot abuse that instrument. This is tricky because I know they are young adults and I understand that they do have and deserve to have social lives. It's just that sometimes their social lives are not the best thing for their instrument. Joking aside the students need to know that it is not healthy to be out until 2AM and then dancing in a class at 8AM. At any age a dancer needs to understand their body's need for real rest in order to maintain and develop an effective instrument. In technique classes I want my students to fully understand the importance of health in their career path. Their body is their livelihood. That is why the word "instrument" describes it so perfectly. Like a musician they need to keep their machine of creation and expression in tune. A dancer's body is her/his guitar or piano. They communicate their inner aesthetic using movement, so the body must be ready to move effectively. Actors need to understand this too. The health of their body determines how well they can physically create a distinct character. If you are an actor playing *The Hunchback of Notre Dame* you are going to have to effectively us your body and reshape it night after night through movement and posture that is foreign to your normal movement. That takes a great deal of energy and care. Proper care of a performing artist's instrument includes nutrition, alignment, health habits, injury treatment, etc. It all affects the dancer or the actor's performance.

*HOW DO YOU APPROACH DEVELOPING A CHARACTER AS A CHOREOGRAPHER AND AS A DANCER?*

I'm an inside-out person. I don't necessarily think, as a choreographer, about how I want my dancers to "look." Instead I encourage them to find their character by experimenting with the emotions that I [as a choreographer] want to come out. I use the techniques of Rudolph Laban, who designed and developed a way to notate dance. His work looks somewhat like a music sheet but the movement is recorded in a different direction on the paper. [To mildly oversimplify, the sheet recordings of Laban Notation read up/down as opposed to left/right to the reader. There is more to it than this, of course, but that is a subject for a different book.] I use creative movement through Laban Techniques as a choreographer. I might tell them to do a movement call a press "closed, low, and slow" and as they do that slow movement I ask them to describe to me what they feel, what emotions are coming out and being created in the individual dancers. I don't approach emotional recall until they can describe what the movement made them feel first. This is how Martha Graham worked when she choreographed. Once they can tell me what they are feeling I ask them to remember a time in their life when they felt that way. I'll have them do a twitching movement and ask them when there was a time they felt that. Then hopefully they will find something in their personal experience that connects and that they can convey. It is abstract; no words to express. Unfortunately for dancers there's a tendency to be external: looking in the mirror, seeing if they are pretty or fully extended. I tell them to connect to the feeling and be real, and the beautiful will follow. Personally as a dancer I approach developing a character the same as I do with my choreography. I like to work "outside/in" and find the emotional core of the character I'm creating through my movement on stage. But when you are the dancer, the one who is being choreographed, it is more of a conversation with the person choreographing the piece. It can be challenging when a choreographer has a different approach than yours. You are the dancer and it is your job to execute their vision. Some of them work very outside-in, relying on you to move the way they ask within the time signatures they set up without much or even any discussion of emotion or story. I've danced for choreographers who don't ever tell you what the piece is about, they just show you the move and ask you to copy it in rhythm to the music. The dancers, even after many performances, may never actually know what the intended message of the work was intended to be. They might never even know if there really was a message or a story being imparted or told. This doesn't necessarily mean that the choreographer has created shallow or ineffective work, by the way. The piece might still be incredibly moving to the people in the audience. While this is not how I work personally, it has worked in many pieces I have danced in. Every dance artist has their own method which has been developed through their training, experience, and point of view. It isn't a question of right or wrong.

*HOW CAN STUDENTS WHO ARE NON-MAJORS OR OTHERWISE NOT NECESSARILY INVOLVED IN THE ARTS BENEFIT FROM LEARNING ABOUT DANCE?*

Here's a great example. I actually work with a lot of the football players. We talk about getting away from all the power being up high in their body so they can get "down into the earth" and be immovable on the field. A lot of the guys are incredibly strong in their upper body but underdeveloped in their legs. This hurts their balance. Heck, I could knock some of them over when I first get them in my class. Of course I don't ... I teach them about center of gravity and the importance of their entire body being flexible and in synch. They are fun and enthusiastic students. Even if you are not a dancer, even if you never dance, your body is still your instrument.

*WHAT IN YOUR OPINION MUST AN INTRO TO THEATRE STUDENT KNOW ABOUT DANCE WHEN THEY LEAVE THE CLASS?*

They should know theatre and dance are different art forms. Both are kinesthetic, but they are very different. Dance is not a piece of theatre; it is its own art. Dance and theatre both are art involving movement and involving the idea that the body is an instrument. After taking the class an Intro to Theatre student should know that both in theatre and dance your movements have to be organic. Those movements have to flow from an emotional place that is found within the artist's character as it is developed during rehearsal. The students should know how both dancers and actors need to have an understanding and awareness of their body as it relates to the space they are in. In other words all performers should know how their body projects feeling and emotion within the confines of a scene or a segment, and literally the space in which the performance is held. If they are in a small black box theatre they will project differently than in an enormous opera house or on an outdoor stage. In either venue they must own the space; and in either case they must be aware how that owning of their space affects fellow performers as well as those watching in the seats. It all has to be a shared experience with the other people onstage. Both dancers and actors need to know the message their movement is giving the audience. Finally I personally don't like when people describe character as being something the performer creates by pretending. I prefer to say that the emotional center of a character, that character's feelings and desires (along with their emotions, both good and bad), at best come from a place inside where they allow themselves to imagine freely.

,

a n Intro to Theatre textbook would do its readers a great disservice if it did not talk about the works and the world of William Shakespeare. Aside from his immense literary and dramatic influence in all of Western culture, Shakespeare's plays remain a source for thousands of jobs every year for theatrical professionals. A quick look at any website regarding the subject will tell you that there are well over one hundred theatre companies dedicated to producing his plays in the United States, Canada, Ireland, and the United Kingdom. This does not even include the companies who are producing his works translated into other languages. On top of that, numerous companies and individual producers, while not dedicated to solely producing Shakespeare plays, will produce one or two in any given season. There is a great deal of work out there doing Shakespeare plays. A stage actor may not consider performing in **Iambic Pentameter** her strongest suit, but if she decides not to train herself to work within the form, she is writing off a large percentage of the roles available in the theatre industry. An actor who says, "I'll never do Shakespeare," is making a very dubious choice. The competition for work

# 17: shakespeare and his theatrical world

onstage in the theatre is extremely tough, and reducing the pool of available jobs so arbitrarily is just bad business.

For designers, the works of William Shakespeare are often a great opportunity, not only for a paycheck, but also to exercise their craft to the edges of their ability. Many Shakespeare plays are produced "**In Period**," which means designing and constructing realistic sets and costumes from the Elizabethan era and times previous. A costume designer creating looks for Romeo and Juliet, for instance, gets the challenge (in a traditional production) of researching the style and dress of Verona in the 15th century. That costume designer then will find color schemes and overall looks that help define the character visually. That visual character created through costume isn't just something the audience gets to appreciate, either. Actors will tell you that, once they get their costumes, a lot of new ideas about their character's movement, emotions, and place in society come forth. The clothes do indeed make the man. Romeo will (in fact, must) have a very different look from his best friend, Mercutio. The warring families of Capulet and Montague would need to have their own distinct styles of dress, color preferences, and insignia. The designers and builders of these costumes would also be charged with making these clothes historically accurate, comfortable, and flexible for the actors (especially characters like Tybalt, Romeo,

*William Shakespeare*

Mercutio, Paris, and the other brawlers who will be doing stage combat with swords) to move in.

The designers, of course, also need to be in synch with the director's concept and the concepts of other designers, such as sets, lighting, and sound—all the while living within the strictures of budget and time. We've used costume design to make the point here, but all of the other designers would find artistically challenging work in the same way. Once again, there are plenty of those jobs to go around working with Shakespeare's plays.

Shakespeare is simply a large part of the world of the modern theatre, from Broadway all the way down to elementary school. The emotions he invokes, the stories he tells, and the characters he creates in his plays make Shakespeare a great night of entertainment, even to audiences that for the most part aren't familiar with a lot of the words and sentence construction they are hearing. Film adaptations like *Ten Things I Hate About You* or *West Side Story* use contemporized versions of his works quite effectively, and many, many films could be named that are adapted from Shakespeare's works.

How can it be that Shakespeare's plays, written as they were for the most part more than 400 years ago, still work for modern theatre audiences? The answer is much simpler than the reader might believe. One of the tragedies of modern American high school students is that all too often they are told they are not sophisticated enough as readers to comprehend Shakespeare's work. This is in no way meant to imply that there are not thousands of wonderful literature teachers working today who do inspire students to enjoy the plays. However, all too frequently, the unfortunate message to emerging students in the United States is that Shakespeare's work is very highbrow poetry that is meant to be analyzed by scholars, not enjoyed as entertainment. Amazingly, nothing could be further from the truth. Shakespeare's language *is* very beautiful and often the imagery *is* very complex, but following the stories he wrote for the stage is easy because Shakespeare himself, in his time, was writing plays for a commercial audience. He meant for those shows to be moneymakers. He uses magic, murder, sex, dirty jokes (including a couple of words that are very controversial to use in public even today), songs, dance, and, of course, gorgeous poetry to make the plays viable entertainment. As brilliant as he was, Shakespeare could not afford to write plays that weren't entertaining and engaging because he had, in Elizabethan London, a lot of very talented competition from some brilliant playwrights for the money that was held in the purses of potential audience members. Playwrights such as Christopher Marlowe, Ben Jonson, and Edmund Spenser (to mention a few of many) were also writing great plays and having them produced. Shakespeare had to appeal to the people in the streets and in the seats or he would have had to find another line of work. There was a lively, and often quite snarky, competition among all of those long-gone writers and actors. The market was quite well served, and maintaining one's share in that market was not an unimportant consideration to a playwright such as William Shakespeare.

Because the plays were written with the intent of being performed for, rather than read by, the audience, it would be ideal if the first exposure that young people in the contemporary Western world got was *seeing a production of a Shakespeare play* rather than examining it as a text in a schoolroom. Fortunately, there are many schools that have the opportunity and budget to do this, but unfortunately there are many who do not. The result is that the reader of this book might be of the opinion that they "hate Shakespeare." This may be true. But the reader is doing a disservice to her- or himself by not going to see a live performance of one of his plays (preferably a "fun" piece like *A Midsummer Night's Dream* or *MacBeth*).

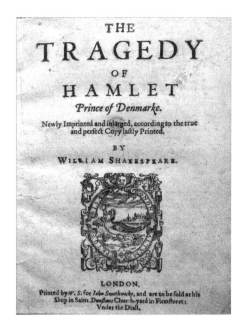

Shakespeare's writing format of iambic pentameter is the subject of a sidebar to this chapter. Read that sidebar because it is an easy way to approach the form used by actors all over the world, and it makes finding the sense of the line easy for even a first-time reader of one of his plays.

So let us look at the way Shakespeare made his plays competitive in the Elizabethan London theatre world. The people in the seats during a performance of a play at that time were separated into two distinct social and economic groups. First, there was the gentry, moneyed, aristocratic people—up to and often including Queen Elizabeth I herself. These upper-class lords and ladies went to the theatre not only to be entertained but to be seen. They would dress beautifully, often paying more attention to the other well-heeled patrons in the theatre than the action onstage. They paid more for their entrance because their accommodations in the space were nicer. They had seats with cushions, shade from the sun (Shakespeare's plays, in his time, were presented in broad daylight), access to food and drink, a better vantage point to the stage, and some coverage over their heads to protect them from the elements. The more a patron paid, the higher up was their seating and the nicer the amenities. It was a juxtaposition of entertainment and societal posturing and politicking; being seen in the best seats let everyone know how affluent, influential, and generally successful you were.

And then there were the groundlings. These people were definitely not upper class, people who today are commonly called "**Blue Collar**." These folks attended the shows as a diversion from their very hard-working lives. They paid a small amount to see the play and for that small amount they were allowed to stand through the performance on the ground in front of the stage. They were thus called **Groundlings** because their accommodations in the theatre were eponymous. Groundlings were more likely to be rowdy and even talk back to the stage. They were not necessarily well dressed. Seeing a play was, in essence, their television or movies. In many accounts of the time they were also referred to as "stinkards," a nickname that apparently was not ironic, especially during the summer.

Shakespeare and his contemporaries wrote their plays to please both of these very diverse audiences simultaneously. That is why *Hamlet* contains not only some of the most riveting poetry in theatrical history but also loads of violence and sex, including a point where Hamlet uses a very naughty word while laying his head in Ophelia's lap. That is why *Hamlet*, and many of Shakespeare's plays, contains sword fighting and murder, while at the same time utilizing themes, references, and imagery gleaned

*William Shakespeare's signature*

Hamlet and the gravediggers *painted by Pascal Dagnan Bouveret, a French painter.*

from classical Greek and Roman mythology and philosophy. Shakespeare (and Marlowe, Jonson, Spenser, et al.) was serving two masters when he addressed his audience. In serving those masters, he was able to create work with a universal appeal. It would, in fact, be very naive to assume that none of the lords and ladies enjoyed the dirty jokes or that none of the groundlings appreciated the poetry and mythology.

So let's look at a day in the life of a typical member of the audience for one of Shakespeare's plays. The growth of cities in the Renaissance, and the growth away from pure subsistence agriculture, began to create a world and a workforce with two very new aspects: disposable income and leisure time. People in the evolving large cities worked an incredibly long day and week to make their living, but compared to eking out an existence on a farm it was a better life with a much greater potential for advancing economically. Working in a city during this period, with its 12-hour workdays and six-day workweeks, provided city dwellers (at least the fortunate ones) time for entertainment and money to spend seeking it. By the time of the Elizabethan era (1558 to 1603), London was an internationally prominent municipality, economically and politically. There was opportunity—which brought Shakespeare there in the first place—to pursue his theatre career.

To demonstrate this time, Shakespeare's heyday, let's invent a typical working-class Londoner and follow him on one of his precious days off. We will call him Nigel. Nigel is an assistant to a blacksmith, and he happens to have a Wednesday off during the theatrical run of the premiere production of *Hamlet*. As he walks toward the theatre, Nigel is offered myriad potential diversions and entertainments. There are taverns, brothels, gambling houses, and inns with all of the amenities aforementioned, along with food. Outside there are loads of places to enjoy a morning and be thrilled. One of the more popular things to see were public executions. The death penalty at this time in England was very liberally meted out. Stealing a purse with more than five pennies in it was a capital offense, for instance. Due to the problems of poverty, unemployment, and illiteracy, there were many common thieves, and stories of boys as young as nine years old being hung for stealing bread were not unheard of. Because these executions were public—and because of the human tendency to engage in Schadenfreude—the hangings were quite popular, and there were many places of execution all over London. Some of these gibbets were quite near the location of the theatres. So Nigel, as he strolls along toward the Globe Theatre, might decide to kill time watching people getting killed. If he was hungry, he might pick up some roasted chestnuts from a vendor on the street to enjoy while he watched some of his unfortunate neighbors have the life choked out of them for swiping a hard roll. People in the gallery watching the hangings would jeer, laugh, and shout clever things at the gallows. In fact, the term "well hung" comes from this phenomenon. The moment a man was hanged, a redistribution of blood in his body would create, well, tangible evidence in the form of a bulge in his clothing. Upon seeing a particularly impressive manifestation people would laugh and shout that the victim was indeed well hung. In almost every case, the victim, while possibly flattered, did not laugh.

After Nigel got bored with watching people get executed, he might still have an hour or two to occupy his time before the play started. He could then enjoy buskers (street musicians and performers, who did everything from singing to magic to tumbling to circus tricks), who would set up in public to attract onlookers in the hopes of being thrown pennies of appreciation for their efforts. Nigel also had the option of enjoying what are now called "animal-based entertainments," such as **Bear Baiting** and **Cock Fighting**. In its most common form, bear baiting consists of chaining a bear to a post and setting dogs on him. The onlookers would bet on this repugnant spectacle, the outcome of their bets depending on whether the bear or the dogs survived. Some bears actually enjoyed long careers at this vicious so-called sport. Cockfighting was essentially the same concept, using roosters which would fight to the death while the audience bet on the winner. The author wants to be very clear about something here. It must be understood that, while the Elizabethan era was a time of rapid economic, educational, and artistic growth, it was still a period that would seem unfathomably brutal to students in the 21st century. The ironic tone being taken while describing our hypothetical Nigel is not meant as an endorsement. It merely is what the cultural landscape was in London around the year 1600. Death was everywhere. Bubonic plague hit London several times a decade. In 1665, almost the entire city burned down. Things were improving, but these were still very hard times.

So finally, after eating his chestnuts, watching his neighbor's execution (and perhaps assessing that neighbor's endowments with an audible bon mot), listening to a singer playing the lute, and watching an animal spectacle, Nigel would be ready to go and see *Hamlet*. If he stood with the groundlings—as he most likely would—he might even engage in some playful heckling of the actors as they portrayed their characters.

That is a day in the life of one of Shakespeare's audience members, specifically "a day off in the life." Shakespeare would reach both Nigel and the Prince of Wales and enthrall them by writing plays that acknowledged both of their desires as consumers of entertainment.

It is this dichotomy that keeps Shakespeare alive as a viable force in modern theatre. The elements of storytelling, humor, drama, action, sex, violence, and the rhythms of language that make poetry resonate are there. He was a genius, not only as a poet and a dramatist, but as a practical businessman as well.

Regardless of what you, the reader, may have been told growing up—whether you had wonderful teachers who ignited in you a love of Shakespeare or misguided instructors who implied to you that his writing was above your head and intellect—you are indeed capable of comprehending and being thrilled by attending a Shakespeare play. That is why there are so very many employment opportunities for theatre professionals in his works.

# breaking down and demystifying iambic pentameter

"IAMBIC PENTAMETER." The very phrase itself often creates a sense of discomfort and disconnection to a modern theatre patron. It seems like something that would soar over the head of the average reader. It sounds a bit like a childhood disease. However, it is actually a simple and elegant form of rhythmic poetry that has been used beautifully in theatre, especially English-language theatre, since the Renaissance. His mastery of this dynamic, rhythmic form is one of the core beauties of William Shakespeare's brilliance as a playwright.

If you ask an actor who is a veteran actor of Shakespeare's plays, she or he will tell you that, even after performing in perhaps dozens of his plays, they do not automatically get the sense of what their character is saying upon a first reading. That actor will tell you that they need to do some analytical work—to "break it down"—not only for their understanding, but in order to communicate the meaning and message to their contemporary audience. Over four centuries, many approaches have been developed to do that breakdown of the text, and the one we will be looking at here is one of the most common and effective techniques around. It is actually easy.

So first, let us demystify the term iambic pentameter. The simple fact is this: Anyone reading this textbook is more than well prepared and intellectually capable of understanding and enjoying plays written in this form. A simple definition of the term is this: Iambic pentameter is writing which has ten syllables per line. An **iamb** is one meter of the line; it is two syllables, and the second syllable gets stressed when speaking it out loud. **Pentameter** merely means that there are five (the **pent** in "pentameter") meters or iambs in the line. When thinking about what stressed and unstressed means, just pick a two-syllable word and say it out loud, giving the second syllable in the word more volume and energy. The likelihood is that you do this frequently in your day-to-day speech with one particular word: "hello." This is especially true when you use that word for sarcastic and comedic effect amongst your friends. Your dormmate or best friend says something you think is kind of dense or silly. You look at that person and say "Hel-LOOOOOOOO!?!"

That sarcastic use of the word hello is iambic. You stress the second syllable to get the point across, that you think your friend's statement was dumb. This is not a stretch on the author's part. It is a legitimate example.

Ten syllables. Five unstressed, and five stressed, with the even numbered syllables in the line getting the most emphasis and the odd numbered syllables getting less emphasis. That's it. It is not **Quantum Physics** or Sanskrit. You, the reader, can find the meaning in some of the most complex speeches in the Shakespeare oeuvre by embracing, rather than running away from, iambic pentameter.

William Shakespeare used the form with incredible grace and effectiveness. When you look at the stressed syllables in his plays, an amazing thing becomes evident. While creating living, breathing, passionate characters and stories, Shakespeare placed the great majority of the information—the preponderance of nouns, action words, and core metaphorical imagery—in the **even-numbered syllables**! This holds true in all of Shakespeare's theatrical works. It is an amazing accomplishment on his part, made even more amazing when you look at the volume of work he created in a comparatively short time.

All a novice reader of a Shakespeare play has to do to find the sense of any particular line or speech, all she or he has to do to get the sense and message of the action, is separate the even-numbered syllables and read them aloud without the odd-numbered/unstressed syllables. This creates lines that sound like they are being spoken by Frankenstein, but those lines make very real sense and hold the meaning contained in the line explicitly.

"To be or not to be. That is the question."

This one sentence is arguably the most widely recognized quote found in any play throughout history. It is a moment of existential crisis, spoken aloud by Hamlet in a soliloquy. No one else is on the stage; he is speaking his deepest and darkest thoughts.

So what does the line mean when stripped down to it essence? What is Hamlet saying, what is Shakespeare saying through him, and what information is the audience intended to receive from this line of poetic dialogue?

Look at the even-numbered syllables.

This is made easier if you put a small case "u" above the unstressed syllables, and a flat line over the stressed syllables. Now read only the words or syllables with the stress line over them. What do you have?

Be      Not     Be      Is      Ques    [tion]

The line is not perfectly iambic, there's that small unstressed –tion at the end, but forget that for now.

Look at the remaining beats in the line. Say them out loud. Say them good and loud.



be not be is question.



Hamlet is torn. He doesn't know if his life is worth continuing. He is questioning whether he wants to continue to exist, to be. The words and syllables that convey this breathtakingly powerful dilemma are contained in the even number syllables, and it continues throughout the entire speech! Later in the soliloquy, he goes on to speculate about what dying literally means. He expresses it thusly:

"To die, to sleep; To sleep: perchance to dream;"

Once again, put a small "u" over the odd numbered syllables and put a "–" over the stressed syllables. Write just the stressed (even-numbered) syllables down and read them loud and clear.

Die       Sleep    Sleep    Chance Dream

Again, Frankenstein talk, and again the pure and powerful sense of the line. Shakespeare, speaking to his audience through the character he has created in the persona of Hamlet, is telling us this:

We perceive death as a form of sleep. Sleep creates the chance that we will dream.

Hamlet goes on to explore what those dreams might be. He isn't able to be completely sure if they will be good dreams or nightmares. In the end, he concludes that his own fear, his internal terror that those death-induced dreams will be something even more horrifying and unbearable than his life on Earth is all that is stopping him from killing himself to end his misery. Otherwise, he says, given the promise of joy in Heaven, and knowing the boredom and suffering and stupidity of life on Earth, why not kill ourselves and start the fun sooner rather than later? He lets us know that religion and social convention stop us from taking the route of self-destruction.

"Thus conscience does make cowards of us all."

That line summarizes why Hamlet is not going to commit suicide, and that line is in iambic pentameter.

Con       Does     Cow      Of All …

The sense of the line, the beauty, depth, and meaning are all there. Iambic pentameter isn't making it harder to get the meaning and understand the sense of the speech. It is, in fact, guiding us to the core words and sounds that take the words on a page and give them life to both the audience and actor.

†he great majority of the ideas and concepts found in this textbook speak to the desire in the world of theatre to create a sense of reality, a sense that the characters portrayed when we see a play are attempting to make those of us in the audience suspend our disbelief and see the action on the stage as a slice of actual life. Believable characters, plotlines with a distinct beginning, middle, and end and dialogue that makes not only sense but has a larger symbolic message are the "norm" in theatre. But art is never entirely about the NORM, is it? At a gallery, we can expect to see paintings by not only realists and illustrators; we can also be assured that on the walls there will be works of Abstraction, Impressionism, Cubism, and Pop Art. The same idea holds true with theatre. After the horrific carnage of World War Two, which followed the horrific carnage of World War One by only 20 years, many playwrights found themselves questioning the veracity and value of concepts such as the well-made play or theatrical truth. Witnesses to and survivors of the Holocaust and the destruction of so many lives and so much property in such a short span of time began to argue that life may indeed have no meaning whatsoever—that there may not be a God with a plan for humanity, that ultimately the only

# 18: theatre of the absurd

reality and meaning a human being could truly lay claim to is whatever she or he was able to tack onto their existence and personal experience. Thus was born the philosophy of **Existentialism**, whose main champion was Jean-Paul Sartre. Sartre, whose treatise on existentialism, *Being and Nothingness*, influences political, philosophical, and artistic thinking to this very day, believed that mankind was caught in a false way of thinking, that humanity was trying to make sense out of a universe that in his mind was intrinsically chaotic. Playwrights, especially those in Europe where the carnage and destruction of the wars was evident everywhere a person could look, took this philosophy and applied it to their work. The absurdist playwrights wrote texts that contained meaningless dialogue, repetitive action, and thought and actions that added to an utter breakdown of all communication and human connection. Absurd plots were written that not only ignored the precepts of Aristotle or the Well-Made Play, but, in fact, smashed those precepts to bits. Reality was something to be scorned and mocked, and playwrights such as Eugène Ionesco, Samuel Beckett, Jean Genet, Harold Pinter, and Tom Stoppard (among many others) made hay and created gut wrenching-drama and belly-wracking laughter in the process of breaking all the conventional rules of theatre. Beckett in particular took on with wicked satire what he saw as the absurdity of believing in a deity. This is demonstrated by this stretch of dialogue in *Waiting for Godot*, in which two of his characters, the impoverished and downtrodden Vladimir and

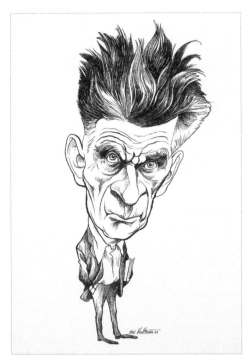

*Caricature of Samuel Beckett, Nobel Prize winner and author of the internationally acclaimed play* Waiting for Godot.

Estragon, discuss the Crucifixion of Jesus Christ and its direct relevance to their situation:

VLADIMIR: Gogo.

ESTRAGON: (irritably). What is it?

VLADIMIR: Did you ever read the Bible?

ESTRAGON: The Bible … I must have taken a look at it.

VLADIMIR: Do you remember the Gospels?

ESTRAGON: I remember the maps of the Holy Land. Coloured they were. Very pretty. The Dead Sea was pale blue. The very look of it made me thirsty. That's where we'll go, I used to say, that's where we'll go for our honeymoon. We'll swim. We'll be happy.

VLADIMIR: You should have been a poet.

ESTRAGON: I was. (Gesture towards his rags.) Isn't that obvious?

VLADIMIR: Where was I … How's your foot?

ESTRAGON: Swelling visibly.

VLADIMIR: Ah yes, the two thieves. Do you remember the story?

ESTRAGON: No.

VLADIMIR: Shall I tell it to you?

ESTRAGON: No.

VLADIMIR: It'll pass the time. (Pause.) Two thieves, crucified at the same time as our Saviour. One—

ESTRAGON: Our what?

VLADIMIR: Our Saviour. Two thieves. One is supposed to have been saved and the other … (he searches for the contrary of saved) … damned.

ESTRAGON: Saved from what?

VLADIMIR: Hell.

ESTRAGON: I'm going. He does not move.

VLADIMIR: And yet … (pause) … how is it—this is not boring you I hope—how is it that of the four Evangelists only one speaks of a thief being saved. The four of them were there—or thereabouts—and only one speaks of a thief being saved. (Pause.) Come on, Gogo, return the ball, can't you, once in a way?

ESTRAGON: (with exaggerated enthusiasm). I find this really most extraordinarily interesting.

VLADIMIR: One out of four. Of the other three, two don't mention any thieves at all and the third says that both of them abused him.

ESTRAGON: Who?

VLADIM What?

ESTRAGON: What's all this about? Abused who?

VLADIMIR: The Saviour.

ESTRAGON: Why?

VLADIMIR: Because he wouldn't save them.

ESTRAGON: From hell?

VLADIMIR: Imbecile! From death.

ESTRAGON: I thought you said hell.

VLADIMIR: From death, from death.

ESTRAGON: Well what of it?

VLADIMIR: Then the two of them must have been damned.

ESTRAGON: And why not?

*Experimental Imagery in the Absurdist Style*

VLADIMIR: But one of the four says that one of the two was saved.

ESTRAGON: Well? They don't agree and that's all there is to it.

VLADIMIR: But all four were there. And only one speaks of a thief being saved. Why believe him rather than the others?

ESTRAGON: Who believes him?

VLADIMIR: Everybody. It's the only version they know.

ESTRAGON: People are bloody ignorant apes.

It can be seen here in this dialogue that these two men speak in roundabout ways that are not unlike the routines of the Marx Brothers or Abbott and Costello. The immortal "Who's on First?" sketch by the latter has this kind of circular talk. Nobody is really listening. Nobody is really communicating. Time is simply passing. As for religious dogma or the possibility of resurrection by a Savior from on high—well, there is scant belief in or hope for that. As Estragon declares at the end of the examination of the Gospels and their discrepancies regarding the story of the thieves, the fact that people tend to believe in the most positive Gospel version of the Crucifixion is not because the universe is fair or that hope at all makes any sense. No; humanity is optimistic because "People are bloody, ignorant apes." This is not a message of hope or an affirmation of the goodness of mankind—it is the observation of a man trapped in a meaningless world where the same events occur over and over again in a mind-numbing repetitive cycle. Everyone in the play is indeed waiting for Godot, and the joke Beckett plays on his audience as well as the characters telling the nonstory is this: Godot never arrives. All we see … is waiting.

The roots of **Absurdist** theatre go back further than the 1950s, of course. Bertolt Brecht had already created theatre that broke convention and did not demand that truth or beauty dominate the stage. To an extent, even the Greek dramatists showed an irreverence for the belief in **Universal Order**, even if their stories ultimately demonstrated the existence of that metaphysical symmetry. In the late 1800s in Paris, the playwright Alfred Jarry scandalized audiences and indeed caused riots with plays such as *Ubu Roi*, which controversially began with the first actor onstage shouting a slurred version of the French scatological profanity, *merde*. Social order in the early 20th century was ready for satire and deconstruction for the same terrible reasons that the entire world descended into war with itself twice: the fabric of classical society was unweaving due to wealth disparity, the ascendance of secularism, the growth and application of new political theories such as socialism, communism, and fascism, and the fading influence of religion as a common base of power.

The term absurdist as a description of the theatrical movement is generally credited to the critic Martin Esslin, who coined it in his essay "Theatre of the Absurd" in 1960. An important influence on the absurdists was the playwright/philosopher Antonin Artaud, who also coined a term, the **Theatre of Cruelty**, that described his belief that theatre should not be afraid to destroy all illusions of reality, not only onstage but in real life. Artaud himself said:

"The Theatre of Cruelty has been created in order to restore to the theatre a passionate and convulsive conception of life, and it is in this sense of violent rigor and extreme condensation of scenic elements that the cruelty on which it is based must be understood. This cruelty, which will be bloody when necessary but not systematically so, can thus be identified with a kind of severe moral purity which is not afraid to pay life the price it must be paid."

*Samuel Beckett's play* Endgame, *performed at Shimer College*

It is indeed an intense mindset. Audiences, much like the audiences witnessing Brecht's epic theatre, were to be shocked and shaken into rejecting their preconceived beliefs. In contrast to Brecht's desire for intellectual examination of belief systems, Artaud went completely the other direction. His belief was that the only way theatre could truly affect an audience was by inducing a visceral, nonverbal reaction. The intellectual complacency lamented by Arturo Ui at the end of Brecht's play, *The Resistible Rise of Arturo Ui*, was to be driven away by symbolic rejection of language itself as a mode of communication. Eugène Ionesco, in his play *The Bald Soprano*, places two couples in a drawing room where they speak meaningless platitudes to each other. Ionesco found his inspiration for the play in a language textbook. Again, the refusal to adhere to any form of plot structure or meaning or discernible story line punctuated Ionesco's personal belief that language itself was a barrier to human communication and interpersonal connection.

Along with this intellectual nihilism, many absurdist writers used the portrayal of death and human suffering as a point to be laughed at. The term for this is **Tragicomedy**, and it is epitomized in Samuel Beckett's *Endgame*, in which the character Nell proclaims, "Nothing is funnier than unhappiness." Once again, the near destruction of the civilized world by two wars and the advent of weapons that could vaporize a city within seconds were affecting theatrical thought. The ripple of this world of despair and meaninglessness was, as culture always has been, reflected in the work of playwrights, directors, and actors. Theatre, in the minds of the absurdists, was to be torn down and rebuilt in the same way the Marshall Plan was used to rebuild many of the bombed edifices of western Europe. Conventions like the fourth wall (which was completely disdained by authors like Luigi Pirandello) and believable stage action were to be thrown away entirely or at least radically redefined. Comforting concepts like linear time lines and coherent storytelling with a discernible moral or lesson would no longer be embraced. Sartre, himself a playwright of no small ability, summed up the pointlessness of existence and the ridiculousness of suffering quite hilariously in his play *No Exit*. As the play ends and the final curtain is about to come down, the character of Garcin comes to realize that the people he is trapped in a room with, his partners in hell, are people he despises. Their mutual punishment is that they all must

*Theatre de la Huchette, Eugene Ionesco, Paris*

spend eternity in each other's intolerable presence. Earlier, Garcin has even gone as far as to state that, "Hell is other people." Now, at the last moment of the script, it becomes obvious that there is, as the title of the play states, no exit from this room and its "other people." At this point, where we most expect him to sink into bottomless despair and perhaps wail to God in rage or for mercy, Garcin simply says, "Well then … Let's get on with it!" Sartre presents people in this play who never expect anything other than suffering. They therefore are characters who see their own tragedy as hilarious. They embody tragicomedy.

Many other philosophies, political concepts, and artistic movements influenced the theatre of the absurd, of course. Indeed, the artistic and intellectual movements of **Surrealism** and **Dadaism** must be acknowledged when talking about this wave of dramatic work. Social trauma, genocide, war, economic collapse, the ascendance of electronic media and communication, as well as the rapid advances of science—all had a hand in creating absurdism and its theatrical proponents. These same stimuli continue to exist all over the Earth in our own era, and because of this the theatre of the absurd will never leave or disappear. Like all movements in art and literature—and, of course, theatre—it will simply evolve until the next Martin Esslin comes along and gives the newest wave of nonrealistic theatre a verbal label.

"'Social change' is a lot to ask, whether it is asked of a theatrical company, its accumulated audience, or for that matter, of any individual playwright. The very word "society" creates the mind space where one looks for their own place within a community and tries to adapt to that placement. Theatre, as we've said several times in this book, reflects the people and historical times of those who create it. The worldview of the Greeks was—and in fact, could only be—a reflection of the philosophy of those times and the human beings who were trying to figure out the world as they knew it. This questioning through art included not only analysis and commentary on the larger world and the universe, but on the single unit that is a person and the inner universe of the human mind. Theatre and art have their value as entertainment and diversion, of course, and the escapism of a good belly laugh or a gorgeous landscape in a painting are not unimportant by any means, but even as far back as the Festival of Dionysus, theatre included a great deal of social commentary. We will later discuss *Lysistrata* and its use of broad sexual humor to ridicule the male reliance upon violence as a method of government and the

# 19: theatre as a conduit for social change

acquisition of wealth. War will always be the cruelest mode of social change. Modern directors and translators stress *Lysistrata*'s antiwar message, and there indeed is a swipe at war in Aristophanes' play, but the bulk of his other plays show the playwright to be somewhat less than a feminist or antiwar thinker by modern standards. Still, the play does talk about the power of women (albeit only through sexual manipulation and extortion) to influence men, and it does ridicule the Peloponnesian War. Yet that ridicule was more a complaint about profiteering and political ineptitude than it was a sentiment we might find in the writings of Gandhi or a John Lennon song.

Politics and art are a tricky mixture to say the least. The authors of this book have tried to remain out of the fray of the **Left/Right** debate or the place of theatre in the economy and government. In the United States, less than 1 percent of the federal budget goes to all of the arts, and theatre is just a wedge of that wedge. On a purely anecdotal level, the authors are based in the city of Buffalo, New York, which has a surprisingly vibrant theatre community for a medium-sized market. Very recently, the city had a quite public debate about whether or not theatre and the arts (which for budgetary considerations were referred to by the governments of the local county and the city itself as "**Culturals**") should receive even one cent of tax money. The sitting **County Executive** emphatically said no, his argument being that theatre doesn't have a tangible fiscal payback

*Bertolt Brecht's grave headstone*

to the community, that it is a "boutique art" enjoyed by a select few aficionados. Local activists in the arts community did a lot of research and found that over 60,000 people a year were coming to see theatre in the city and that their financial contribution to the ancillary neighborhood businesses like restaurants and taverns could be conservatively estimated to be close to one million dollars. The argument was also made that in a Rust Belt city with chronic underemployment, culture was an invaluable attraction to potential new business. Research shows that when recruiting employees, new industry looks to paint their location as a desirable place to work with a high quality of life in order to attract people who are at the top of their careers. Those higher-end workers generally look at culture as an important piece in the quality-of-life mosaic. In the end, the county executive who proposed cutting theatre and the arts from the budget failed in his reelection bid; a great deal of the exit polls showed that this controversy was a major contributor to his demise at the ballot box. In short, the arts are controversial politically. The culture of America feels passionately on both sides regarding the question of public funding for theatre. And this is true not only in Buffalo, New York, but in municipalities across the nation.

The arguments for and against government funding of the arts is not peculiar to America, either. All nations, including those that fund their theatres at a higher percentage than the United States, ask this question: How much input into creative content does the government desire/deserve/demand for their money? Artistic freedom and its relationship to public funding is not an easy yes or no argument. Censorship is always a threat to all expression. "State-run" theatres and galleries worldwide contain and create some breathtaking work, but they also contain works that are bald propaganda. So, again: Should government be in the theatre or arts business? Maybe not. But on the other hand, is the role of government only to build roads, schools, sewers, and the machinery of war? We will leave it to the reader to make up his or her mind on this part of the puzzle.

Voltaire, who was not only a playwright but a philosopher and novelist, took France, his nation, to task for its cruelty and indifference to suffering and poverty. In *Candide*, he continually has the affluent, ignorant, and the clergy proclaiming that this is "the best of all possible worlds" in the face of terrible tragedy. His point was that inaction and indifference and false optimism are not passive in the equation of suffering: they actively contribute to it.

But theatre is intrinsically political, isn't it? Even *Romeo and Juliet* speaks to the issue of blind hatred, which is why it provided such an excellent template for *West Side Story* and its social commentary about American crime, assimilation of immigrants, and the ascendance of street gangs in major cities in the United States.

As with the next chapter, "Theatre History," we could write tens of thousands of words about theatre as a conduit of cultural change. Therefore, as with that chapter, we will once again cherry-pick without apology, all the while encouraging the reader to research and argue any and all ideas presented.

So here is a selected and selective list of playwrights whose overt politics were culture changers and challengers, with no regard necessarily for timeline or the effectiveness over the longer test of time of their works.

Bertolt Brecht was truly a political theatre giant in many ways, as well as being a proponent of theories regarding acting and playwriting that were radical in his time and arguably still are in the present. Brecht lived through incredibly tumultuous political times in his native Germany and the world, including both World Wars. His personal politics were Marxist, causing him to be **Blacklisted** by the House Un-American Activities Committee in the United States, from the late 1940s until his death in 1956. These blacklistings took place during what is often referred to as The McCarthy Era." Brecht proposed a concept called Epic Theatre, which espoused that the audience should not be asked to identify emotionally with the characters on the stage. Brecht wanted audiences to *think*. He felt that emotional connection and empathy for what were, of course, merely actors pretending to be another human being and pretending to live a scenario that was in no way a real historical event, per se, made the viewer intellectually lazy. Brecht wanted the audience, at all times, to be aware that they were NOT witnessing reality. He wanted them to see that the characters onstage were actors with a sociopolitical message, and ultimately Brecht believed that it was the purpose of theatre to point out the cruelty and injustice of society and governments. He wanted the people in the seats to be challenged to *think and rationally examine their world and their place within it*. In 1941, Bertolt Brecht wrote a scathing criticism of the Western world based upon the ascendance of Adolph Hitler called, *The Resistable Rise of Arturo Ui*, which brilliantly demonstrated this **Epic Theatre** style. The title character, Arturo Ui, is a Chicago gangster who tries to take over the control and access to the **Cauliflower Racket**. Portrayal of a banal vegetable such as cauliflower as a highly desired and lucrative commodity, worthy of murder in the pursuit of market control, was a satirical stroke of genius. His fellow gangsters, as well as his gangland rivals, are all based upon the actual people who ran the Third Reich. The gangster allegory is resonant of the way in which Hitler and those around him took control of not only Germany but almost the entire world, while well-meaning citizens of Europe and America watched without intervening. It is both funny and poignant. Brecht wrote *Ui* in 1941, although it wasn't actually produced on stage anywhere until the late 1950s. At the very end of the play, Brecht gives the actor portraying Ui a speech to deliver, out of character and as the individual human being that the actor is instead of as Ui. This is said directly to the audience, person to person, performer to spectator, with no pretense that the story that has just been acted was real in any sense:

> "If we could learn to look instead of gawking,
>
> We'd see the horror in the heart of farce,
>
> If only we could act instead of talking,

We wouldn't always end up on our arse.

This was the thing that nearly had us mastered.

Don't rejoice in his defeat, you men!

Although the world stood up and stopped the bastard,

The bitch that bore him is in heat again."

This is not only quite a challenge to those in the seats, it is downright frightening to a modern viewer to see how prescient Brecht truly was. Writing in 1941, a time when Hitler looked invincible, Brecht predicted his defeat while simultaneously predicting that the bitch that makes killers like him—the greed and hatred, along with the complacency of humanity— would create new fomenters of evil and genocide. It is believed that Brecht never saw the play onstage.

Genocide is quite a heady topic for a theatre to go after, but playwrights such as Athol Fugard wrote scathing plays exposing the cruelty of South Africa's racist system of Apartheid, such as *Master Harold and the Boys* and *Statements After an Arrest Under the Immorality Act*. *Statements* uses the language of passionate love between a black man and a white woman, who meet secretly to share their dreams and yes, make love. The couple create an interracial mixture that was illegal and vigorously prosecuted in South Africa during the **Apartheid** years. Both lovers meet in a discreet and simple hut and are naked, for obvious symbolic reasons, during the entire play. At the end, they are arrested. Plays like this made Fugard a symbol of great decency and courage, especially since, as a Caucasian citizen of the nation, he was in effect calling for the end of a system that made him automatically a member of the empowered class. Many of his fellow citizens considered him a traitor to his race because of this, and he was (although hopefully no longer is) no stranger to death threats.

Candide *by Voltaire*

The writings of female playwrights such as Eve Ensler, Sara Ruhl, Hattie Gossett, among scores of others, have brought feminist and humanitarian issues, ranging from sexual and reproductive rights to economic and cultural equality to the stage, especially in the 20th and 21st centuries. Ensler's *Vagina Monologues*, an often hilarious and concurrently heartbreaking work, enjoys almost constant production all over the world. Many colleges, arts organizations, and political groups come together every February 14th to celebrate "V Day" with readings and full productions of this script, which is a series of monologues in which women of all ages and backgrounds talk about their relationship to and the power of owning their genitalia without shame. Critics in many media have pointed out that this script is not only breathtakingly honest and an important starting point for adult conversation about significant issues such as gender identity, but it is also an educational manifesto about what it means to be a woman. This work often leaves male audience members squirming in recognition of their own biases and cultural ignorance regarding what Shakespeare and many others referred to as "the weaker sex."

People of color, the poor, victims of persecution and violence, and all groups and individuals that fall under the category described as the disenfranchised, have traditionally used theatre as an outlet and medium of expression. During the Cold War, playwrights such as Slawomir Mroczek risked incarceration—or worse—for performances of their works, which often were held in private homes to avoid the attention of the state and its police. These plays, such as Mroczek's renowned *They*, used abstract writing and the language of absurdism to not only skewer their totalitarian governments, but also as a means to present their message between

The Vagina Monologues *by Eve Ensler, performed by San Fran Annie*

the lines right under the noses of the forces of suppression. A truly remarkable development occurred, in which the art of theatre itself became the springboard to national leadership. Václav Havel, the Czech playwright and political dissident, became in 1989 the last president of Czechoslovakia, and the first president of the new Czech Republic in 1993. Havel had used his prowess as an intellectual and theatrical writer to voice his conscience worldwide in his triumphant 1960s plays *The Garden Party* and *The Memorandum*. In his lifetime, Havel won numerous humanitarian awards, all the while demonstrating that theatre, the arts, and politics need not be adversaries but, in fact, can complement each other for the greater good of humanity.

Because theatre is live, and because it not only depends upon but demands the presence and emotional/intellectual involvement of an audience, it will always remain an important communication tool for exploring or advocating new politics, critical thinking, social problems, and solutions to those problems. Because each performance of any play is an ephemeral one-time event, it has an elasticity and life that allows it to comment upon and influence the entire world. The authors fervently hope that the readers of this text take this previous statement to heart and use their own creativity to shape a better world. It may sound sentimental to make such a statement, but sentimentality does not automatically disqualify the importance of being involved in improving society.

Stage versions of *The Diary of Anne Frank* have brought the ugly realities of the Holocaust of World War Two to light for many audiences worldwide. An experimental 2006 production of the play, in which Anne's story is simultaneously portrayed along with an allegorical Anne who is being hunted down during the Rwanda genocide of the mid 1990s, led to an annual conference known as "the Anne Frank Project." The project explores the responsibility of those who create art, especially theatre, to change the culture of the world and prevent future genocides through exploration of the roots of such violent explosions of hatred and violence. Here is the mission statement of this conference, which first was held in 2009. It has since become a truly international event, with live Internet hookups to several nations on several continents:

"The **mission** of *The Anne Frank Project* is to encourage communities to utilize the words and wisdom of Anne Frank as a starting point for the intense examination of genocide, intolerance, bigotry and racism as a means towards finding solutions towards an elevated and shared human condition.

Multiple local, national and international initiatives will provide a forum for:

Exploring the impact of Anne Frank's ideals throughout history, cultures and diverse populations.

Exploring genocide from a variety of disciplines and perspectives.

Exploring current education practices in Holocaust, genocide and tolerance studies.

Exploring the power of *storytelling* as a primary vehicle for social justice and community reparation.

Honoring the life and wisdom of the countless victims of genocide, hatred and intolerance.

Activating the reality of our *Shared Humanity*.

The **vision** of *The Anne Frank Project* is to provide the world with the necessary tools and vocabulary to activate the forgiveness, unity and peace processes. Arming the world with these new tools will remove the role of *bystander* from any conflict."

If the reader desires to participate in the Anne Frank Project, or for that matter any project for the betterment of our world, here is a link that will give you a good start:

*www.theannefrankproject.com*

It would be folly to try to cover the idea of Theatre History in one chapter or for that matter even in one book. The bibliography of this subject gives any laptop owner thousands of hits with a simple Google search. So how do we cover the ideas an Intro to Theatre student should know about this subject, with specifics, when the very nature of doing so in one chapter says we must be cherry picking our examples out of myriad possibilities? Our answer is simple: we are indeed going to cherry pick and without apology. The reader is welcome to follow up on our statements if they are so inspired (which is genuinely the hope of the Authors) with their own reading. For purposes of clarity we will give an Overview in this chapter, and then break the chapter into two parts: Theatre in Ancient Times, and Theatre in Modern Times. One concept must be grasped fully before the Authors move on with this segment of the text: Theatre has, does, and always will both reflect and be influenced by the society that creates it. Conversely, Political, Cultural, and Philosophical movements throughout history have been influenced by Theatre and vice-versa.

# 20: theatre history

## OVERVIEW

When looking at the history of theatre or any other art it is important to understand that it is a continuum: theatre has developed over time with past styles and approaches having influence over the newer styles and approaches. When we talk about the theatre of Ancient Greece or Rome we are talking about the great-great grandparents of what we see on stage today. Even the forms of theatre that rebel against classic (or simply previous) forms wouldn't exist if there were *no previous forms to rebel against*. To put it another way: you do not get Rock and Roll music without first having Country and Rhythm and Blues. Artistic expression builds and evolves over time, and the newer artists tend to begin their pursuit by looking at what has come before. This continuous line through time is why Theatre History matters a great deal to the modern theatre. Once again, it would be foolish for a Playwright or an Actor or a Director not to avail themselves to the knowledge, or even the mistakes, of previous creative people in the time line. It is not uncommon for newer Theatre Artists to look at their antecedents like a buffet from which they pick only what they like or works for their vision. So let us look at the Historical Buffet beginning with Ancient Theatre.

# THEATRE HISTORY IN ANTIQUITY

The oldest plays, the oldest existing theatrical works that are currently available to us, come from the Greeks. This is not in any way to imply that there were not theatrical forms of storytelling or entertainment or religious ritual before the Ancient Greeks. Storytelling and the Oral Tradition are as old as the concept of language itself. Many faculty members reading the preceding sentences would be quick to argue that in fact the oldest Theatre was performed in Egypt as part of their worship, especially the Osiris Passion Play which was performed annually for over 2000 years. These religious festivals were, according to Egyptologists, theatrical and storytelling in nature and therefore have a meaningful place on the timeline. However it is important to draw a distinction here. No modern theatre-goer would recognize these works as anything resembling what is now called a "play." The Osiris Passion Play typically lasted for days and occasionally included actual human sacrifices. Religious ritual has its own history and place, and *yes—it has influenced theatrical storytelling*, but it is more of an influence than an example of theatre. The authors of this book do not consider this to be the end of the argument, the distinction could be argued for quite a long time and in fact it has indeed been argued for centuries. Please feel free to avail yourself of the reading on this subject if this argument, as it probably does, intrigues you. This text is working with the premise that the oldest writings recognizable as plays go back to the ascendance of the Grecian Empire. Therefore, let's get back to the Greeks.

Around the middle of the 6<sup>th</sup> Century BCE, the City Dionysia was annually held in the city of Athens to honor Dionysus, the God of Fertility and Wine. This festival featured a playwriting competition. Three tragic playwrights would compete for the prize. They were required to present three tragedies per writer, along with what was known as a "Satyr Play" which was a form of comedy that often included themes of sexual promiscuity and slapstick comedy. In their theatre the Greeks were anything but shy about sex, in fact they often would portray sexu-

*Greek theatre in Syracuse*

ally aroused men using enormous fake male genitalia which were each individually known as a *phallus*. Themes of infidelity, stupidity, greed, and senseless violence were part and parcel to the comedic workings found in Satyr Plays. The reader, when giving this idea some thought, may come to see that these themes, these emotions and human foibles, remain the basis of comedy to the present day. It is in fact our oversized appetites and our lower emotional instincts that make us laugh. These plays also were forums in which satire of the social situation and political landscape was explored. The brilliant Aristophanes comedy "Lysistrata" is a prime example. In this play, the women of Athens, weary of the suffering, deprivation, and loneliness caused by the **Peloponnesian War** between Sparta and Athens (which lasted from 431 to 404 BCE) unite to deny sex to their husbands until they find a way to end the hostilities. By the end of "Lysistrata" the men on both sides are literally unable to carry their blood swollen sexual members and in fact do indeed agree to sue for peace; the moral being that, given the choice between violence and sexual pleasure, men will generally choose the latter. Both the poignancy of this play and its amazing depth of genuine humor remain real for audiences even in modern times. In fact a worldwide series of staged readings of "Lysistrata" were held simultaneously across the world by women in early 2003 as a protest against the forthcoming US invasion of Iraq.

*Roman theatre ruins in Albania*

The surviving plays of the Ancient Greek Theatre were written by four playwrights: Aristophanes, Aeschylus, Sophocles, and Euripides. These include 31 tragedies by three, possibly four playwrights ("Prometheus" is no longer thought to be written by Aeschylus) and 11 comedies by Aristophanes. Seven tragedies were by Sophocles and 17, with the addition of a satyr play, by Euripidies.

Of course these four men were not the only playwrights of the region and the era, but unfortunately only their writings have been preserved as of the writing of this book. Perhaps in coming days there will be an archaeological find that brings out the works of more playwrights from this era; it is something to hope for. All four of these playwrights created theatrical works that are still being produced. The prevalent themes of their plays were the mythology of Classical Greek culture and the religious narrative that formed the basis of Grecian theology. Although the majority of plays from these four authors were mythology inspired, the oldest existing script that has been found was based on what was then recent history. That play is "The Persians" by Aeschylus.

The end of the Classical Greek period saw theatre coming of age in the great Empire of Ancient Rome. Greece, and its culture, did not disappear of course. Like many nations and cultures they were enveloped and assimilated into the Roman Empire. When looking back at the Romans as a cultural entity an individual quickly notices that much of the theology, mythology, and art of the Greeks were co-opted into the Roman milieu. For example Ares, the Greek God of War, became Mars, the Roman God of War. Zeus, the King of the Greek Gods, became Jupiter, the Roman King of Deities. In similar fashion the playwriting style, form, and inspiration for content of the Roman Theatre was essentially borrowed from the Greeks. The Romans simply made it their own. With their immense wealth and admiration of the spectacular in art, architecture, and literature, what the Romans added to the mix in theatre history can be seen in the many spectacular theatres which were built during their era. The general opinion found among scholars, the consensus (but again we warn that consensus among scholars does not automatically equal fact or the end of argument or research) about Roman Theatre is this: it had a tendency, when compared to the literary theatrical works of the classic Greek Playwrights, to skew more towards entertainment and pleasing the masses. The Satyr influence, the bawdy and violent imagery and storylines which were only a minority theme in the Greek Theatre were in fact the majority in the Roman Theatre. The Romans were generally more concerned, when presenting theatre, with entertaining their audience. This of course doesn't mean that there were no serious Roman dramas or works that examined deeper questions of the human comedy. The more literary and dramatic/tragic works of the Roman Theatre were generally not presented as plays which were acted out on stage but rather as readings to be heard and contemplated by their audience. Examinations of mankind and the place of humanity within the framework of the universe were not entirely beyond the Romans. It just so happens that, when it came to going out for a day's amusement, these questions were not necessarily foremost on the Roman entertainment consumer's mind. The Roman poet and philosopher Juvenal summed this reality up quite effectively when he said, in speaking of the mass of middle and lower class citizens in the Roman Empire: "Give them Bread and Circuses and they'll never revolt." Juvenal's point was, of course, that people are often contained from revolt or demands for societal reform by entertainment and the fulfillment of their most basic needs. This is a particularly cynical point of view toward the average working man or woman, but echoes of Juvenal's argument are certainly relevant in modern times. Affordable pizza delivery, and a flat screen television, can be argued to be all an average American needs in order to be placated in this era.

The Roman Empire came to an end, after a long decline, in the year 476 ACE. It was in that year that the last Roman Emperor was deposed and replaced by a Germanic ruler named Odoacer. European culture, especially the Arts, essentially went underground, was assimilated into religious rites and edifices, or fell into the hand of scattered small entities with no central theme or culture as a core. Troupes of itinerant performers would travel from town to town seeking a subsistence living, literally performing from the back of horse drawn carts. There were, as well, religious pageants and theatricals. In the course of spreading the Christian Religion to a largely Pagan and almost entirely illiterate populace, the use of theatre to tell the stories of the developing Bible were of great use to the nascent Church of Rome. With often quite comical effect these tales would include slapstick comedy and even bawdy humor to tell such reverent stories as the Arrival of the Magi. Professor Donn Youngstrom has referred to some of these plays, specifically, "The Second Shepherd's Play" without being inauthentic, as being "The Three Stooges Meet The Virgin Mary." Students who major in either Theatre or Literature are often shocked by this irreverence when they read these plays, but remember that humor has always been considered one of the most effective ways to spread a message or advertise an idea.

Phrases like "The Dark Ages" and "The Middle Ages" conjure up a lot of notions when the reader sees them. From King Arthur to the Canterbury Tales; Beowulf to the Decameron, the literary and dramatic works of these periods has an aura of the past, a sense of the no longer existent tenets of Chivalry or Monarchic Rule when they are considered by many in the present age. The wars, plagues, religious disputes, and economic hardship of these largely tribal times in Western Europe did indeed lead to what might seem a break in the continuum of theatre History. The rise of the Italian City States and the Merchant Classes were just one of many historical factors that, during the late 14th and early 15th Centuries, ushered in a new blooming of art and culture that define what this text is referring to when we talk about the Modern Age of Theatre History. This Italian rebirth was the beginning and it spread throughout Europe eventually, becoming known, as a general time period, as The Renaissance.

# MODERN THEATRE HISTORY

"The Renaissance." This Phrase has a beautiful ring to it, and the word Renaissance itself is still commonly used by many people to describe a time of improvement or an era of positive change. For all of the arts including Theatre, the Renaissance was indeed (as the word itself means) a rebirth.

Stylistically, the Renaissance introduced a theatrical and literary concept known as NEOCLASSICISM which was based upon the writings of Horace's "The Art Of Poetry" as well as the "Poetics" of Aristotle. While "The Art Of Poetry" was reasonably well known among Academic literary circles, "The Poetics" was relatively unknown prior to the end of the 15th Century and was not translated into Italian (an important distinction since the Renaissance, while a movement that ultimately swept all of Europe, was initially an Italian cultural phenomenon: Italy led the way in other words) until 1549. Neoclassicism would be the prominent form of theatrical style from the latter 16th Century until at least the mid-18th Century, with many scholars of the opinion that Neoclassicism dominated right up until the French Revolution in 1789.

So what, practically, from the standpoint of theatre, is Neoclassicism? It falls into four main rules or precepts that were to be expected of good theatre:

First, plays were expected to strive for **Verisimilitude**: The appearance of truth. Verisimilitude was divided into three sub categories:

1. Reality. A play was expected to be constructed of events that *could actually happen*. This meant that there would be no soliloquies, ghosts or other supernatural characters, no chorus, and no battles/crowd scenes that were impossible to make look real onstage.

2. Morality. Wickedness must be punished, good must prevail, and those who are good must be rewarded by the end of the play.

3. Universality. Regardless of the time period of the play, the morals and ethics defined by Reality and Morality, must be demonstrated to have been true throughout all of human history, therefore reaffirming that the good and bad qualities of human behavior have always been consistent, which equated theatrical truth.

Second, Plays were expected to follow the rules of **Decorum**. Humanity, and the interactions between characters onstage, were expected to follow the laws of society. Royalty was categorized and depicted as the pinnacle and portrayed with a respect of the social order that worked all the way down from the Throne to the gutter, and societal roles for each rank (including not only social status but age, sex, and profession) were not to be challenged: The Class System was to be presented with respect and celebrated in art.

Third, Plays were subject to a concept known as **The Unities**. Plays were to have one plot; no subplots, and ideally this plot was a story that took place in no longer than a 24 hour period. As to this time restraint, there were writers and academicians who argued that the action of a play should include only events that could have occurred in a twelve hour real-time period.

Fourth, Plays were expected to adhere strictly to **Genres**. Comedy was to show only lower and middle class characters (since of course, the Upper Classes would never be ridiculous …) Comedy had to have a happy ending and be written in prose. Tragedy must deal with the plights of those occupying the upper classes; written in verse and with an ending that was (as the name of the genre itself states) tragic. The law of Genre can be simply stated thusly: No mixing of genres (and therefore the implication that the Class System could be considered something less than a sacrosanct truth) was allowed.

In Italy during the Renaissance the most popular form of theatre was known as the Commedia dell' arte (roughly translated as "the comedy of professional artists".) There were similar but significantly different forms as well, notably Commedia all'improviso (or improvised comedy), Commedia a sogetto (comedy developed from a pre-chosen plot, theme, or subject), and Commedia erudita ("learned or educated" comedy.) All'improviso, a sogetto, and erudite, were performance forms usually presented by amateurs at Court or at academies. Commedia dell' arte was theatre performed by professional troupes. Not entirely unscripted; the shows were improvised by the actors following a plot line posted backstage. There are over 1000 plotlines that survive from the period between 1545 and 1610. Later, in the 18th Century, full length and fully scripted plays were developed from many of these scenarios.

In general Commedia dell' arte featured a broad variety of comic portrayals and included always the use of Stock Characters. These Stock Characters represented all aspects of society and their main function was to serve as the target of lampoon. The actors utilized classic bits of comic business (things like pratfalls and gestures and all sorts of physical and verbal comedic actions) which were referred to as Lazzi. All levels of society were fair game for ridicule in the Commedia. Stock Characters broke down into three main categories: **Masters, Servants, and Young Lovers** with sub categories within. These sub-categorical characters had traditional formal names. Among the Masters you would find the characters Capitano, Pantalone, and Dottore. Among the servants? Arlecchino (Harlequin), Brighello (Sometimes called Scaramouche or Scapino), Pulchinetto (Punch), and Pierrot. Also among the servants was a significant type of character called a *fantesca*, (whose prime example is the character Columbine.

These stock characters heavily influenced playwrights in many nations, in fact to this very day. Shakespeare used many tropes and characters that fit within the influence of commedia, especially in his comedies. The incredibly hilarious character of Malvolio in Twelfth Night, a pompous and scheming man who ends up the victim of an utterly humiliating come-uppance in the final act of the play, is very much a Commedia inspired character. Moliere, the great 17th Century French playwright and social commentator, used doctors in many of his plays, usually to sardonic comic effect. A splendid example of this would be the quack doctor and his idiot physician son in "The Imaginary Invalid." These two charlatans are absolutely recognizable incarnations of Il Dottore who swindle, misdiagnose, and give constant "cures" (including multiple enemas) to a man who is not at all truly sick but rather an eccentric and overly privileged hypochondriac. The Marx Brothers, the Three Stooges, Even the characters in Family Guy or The Simpsons have their roots in this comedic tradition.

Concurrently with the rise of Commedia, the Italian Renaissance saw the rise of Opera. Opera is well represented in the performing arts in current times, with companies let The Metropolitan Opera in New York and many others drawing consistent audiences to their productions all around the world.

During the 16th Century, as England fully embraced the spirit and advances of the Renaissance, theatre bloomed like a field of poppies after a soaking spring rain. A full time theatre space, *The Red Lion,* opened in London in 1547 and it ushered in an age of great popularity for theatre as a form of art and entertainment. By the end of the 1500's London had an extraordinarily thriving theatrical scene. Not only was William Shakespeare in his prime as a Playwright, Actor, and Producer (he was in fact one of the owners of the Globe Theatre; the venue in which many of his plays first were seen), this great *salon* of artists included other star playwrights such as Ben Jonson and Christopher Marlowe among many others. Notable actors of the era include Richard Burbage (for whom it is commonly believed Shakespeare specifically wrote the role of Hamlet), John Heminge (who is believed to be the first to play the great comedic character Falstaff), and Nathan Field (the actor who purportedly replaced Shakespeare himself within The King's Men, the great theatrical troupe of the time.) This golden age lasted just shy of 100 years, until it was abruptly ended by the rise of the Puritans, who, under the leadership of Oliver Cromwell, banned the theatre entirely as being sinful. This proscription lasted until the Restoration eighteen years later in 1660, when Charles II returned the Monarchy to power in England and the theatres were reopened. The English Renaissance in theatre, pre-1642, featured a return to the use of mythology, mysticism, poetic allegory, and a general re-embracement of the tenets of theatre proposed and adhered to by the Greek and Roman arts of the Ancient Classic Age. Themes such as loyalty to monarchy, man's subjection to God, and the triumph (or at least domination by) emotion and active feeling over reason, logic, and ultimately chaos, were at the forefront of these playwrights and their plays, and the adherence to Celestial Order, especially in the context of loyalty to one's rulers, was assumed to be at the core of human decency. In France, the mid to late 1600's saw the emergence of Moliere, whose comedies were based upon often wicked satire, along with slapstick scenarios, of the upper middle and affluent classes. Both Shakespeare and Moliere, and the majority of their theatrical contemporaries, were however largely more interested in using satire not as a tool of societal change per se; but rather as a way to gently nudge the ruling classes and tease them about their occasional hypocrisy. They weren't necessarily dramatists who desired to rework the world order, they were commenting from the inside on a culture they largely saw as advanced and beneficial to all.

Then, in the world of thought, literature, and art, a revolution evolved.

After the Restoration in England, and in in fact all over Europe as well as the American Colonies, the late 17th Century saw the rise of what has come to be known as "The Enlightenment" or "The Age Of Reason." Philosophers such as Spinoza, Voltaire, and John Locke; along with the rise of Empirical Science, which was fathered by Pre-Enlightenment scientists like Da Vinci, Copernicus, Galileo, and Kepler, saw a flowering that led to the breakthrough scientific theories of Isaac Newton. This groundbreaking theorist

*The Old Globe Theatre*

and experimentalist, who explained the force of gravity, the science of optics, and the language of higher math that came to be called Calculus, is the epitome of an Enlightenment thinker. All of these scientific and mathematical breakthroughs were born through experiment; through empirical research techniques that we now know as The Scientific Method. Newton is merely the most famous example of the scientific enlightenment of this period. For instance, while Newton is often credited with the "invention" of Calculus, the first book written explaining this higher mathematical form was published in Germany by Leibniz. The question of who actually "created" Calculus is a matter of heated debate to this present day. This explosion of thought was centered upon a philosophical adherence to the power of reason over the power of religious dogma, superstition, and absolute Monarchy. The most controversial aspect of The Enlightenment was its exploration of the heretical notion that the universe might be ruled by physical/natural laws as opposed to the whims of a specific Deity. This of course led to a similar revolution in Theatre. The basis of contemporary thought during the Enlightenment was based on the precept that dialog, education, rational (non-emotional) thought, and the separation of culture from religion (up to and including in government) was a superior approach to society and its imperfections. Mankind was going to think and reason and experiment its way into a better, more equitable and humane, society. French philosopher/Playwrights such as the afore-mentioned Voltaire along with dramatists such as Beaumarchais took the application of reason and logic to such great lengths that both suffered a fair amount of persecution by members of the Bourgeois Aristocracy; an Aristocracy that found itself quite often portrayed in fashions that were less than flattering in the works of these artists. Voltaire adapted "Oedipus Rex" by the Classic Greek playwright Sophocles and applied rational thought and motivations to its characters; Beaumarchais gave the world "The Marriage of Figaro" and "The Barber of Seville". Both playwrights, among many others, experienced suppression of their writings.

The Enlightenment demonstrates, in its thinking toward Theatre and Philosophy and Art, the tendency of History in general to swing between movements like a pendulum. For Theatre History this meant a swing away from the intellectual and rational approach of the Enlightenment back towards the "Classic" forms of Theatre and their focus on themes of beauty and universal order. Thus, concurrently in many cases, The Enlightenment led to a stage of Theatrical (and artistic) evolution that has come to be known as "Neo-Classicism." Indeed there were already Neo-Classical Playwrights in France during the Enlightenment. History moves forward in fits and starts and sometimes simultaneously until one form takes precedence. It can be confus-ing; remember that it is a Continuum-not a Straight Line. As the term states rather directly, Neo-Classicism was a movement away from strict adherence to the intellect and science and back towards moral ideals and the portrayal of natural beauty. The foundations of Neo-Classic philosophy were based upon the need for man to accept a place in society, culture, and nature itself that put the needs of the individual second to the needs of the many. It was time, once again, to put God back at the top of everything, be humble, and follow your leaders (whether religious, economic, or political) for the good of your nation. It was time to know, and accept, your place in the social strata. The apotheosis of this swing from the Rational to the Neo-Classic led to a period of theatre, especially in England, known as Restoration Comedy. These were dramatic stories with a great deal of humor in which members of the middle classes were sub-jected to mild parody for humorous purposes, but overall these middle class citizens were seen as people to be admired, respected, and aspired to by those of lower station. Englishmen Oliver Goldsmith and Richard Brinsley Sheridan have left modern theatre-goers with many works that fit this category of play, which was known as "Middle Class Drama" or "Domestic Drama." These include Sheridan's "School For Scandal" and Goldsmith's "She Stoops To Conquer" among many other works not only by this duo but many of their dramatic contemporaries.

Western Theatre History, as the 18th Century grew into the 19th Century, is a study in various movements and styles depending upon which country you speak of. In England, there was resurgence in the performing of Shakespeare's plays, which, during the 17th and 18th Centuries were not only marginalized, but even edited with rewritten story lines and endings. A particularly notorious rewrite that was occasionally performed actually had Romeo and Juliet live happily ever after at the end. 19th Century England also saw a great rise in popularity of Melodrama, (a form of theatre that was heavily influenced by, as we shall see in the next paragraph, theatre in France) along with the ascendance of Music Hall entertainment and Light Operetta. Both the Light Operetta and Music Hall (variety) shows laid the groundwork, along with the ascendance in the late 1800's of Vaudeville in the United States, for the Musical Theatre that is now a staple on the West End of London, Broadway in New York, and all around the world.

*Vaudeville poster*

France, as mentioned earlier, was a place where melodrama flourished. A modern reader is unlikely to think of Melodrama as a flattering epithet. Melodrama is a much derided form, and was even during this time, for its dependence on stereotypes, stock emotional situations, and heavy reliance on simplistic interpretations of morality and theology. It was, however, in the Egalitarian spirit of Post Revolution France, very popular as it tended to portray the so called "common man" favorably overall.

Both German and French Theatre in the 19th Century embraced, at least for a time, a form of expression known as Romanticism. German playwrights such as Goethe and Schiller extolled the virtues of national pride as well as a belief that feeling and instinct, rather than rational thought, were the doorways to living a morally admirable life. The French playwrights who worked within the Romantic idiom (a form which generally followed a philosophy that was embodied in the writings of Emmanuel Kant) including Victor Hugo and Alexandre Dumas.

Kant's premise regarding art and theatre was thus: the value of Art (from the Romanticist's point of view) came from its unique capability of giving eternal truth, and the beauty of eternal truth, a form which was concrete. Romantic Art and Theatre was tangible. It could be seen and contemplated by mankind and thus had the power to inform and inspire. Kant saw the arts as a guide to the individual human being allowing her/him an insight into the meaning of Truth and Beauty in the higher metaphysical sense.

The United States during the 1800's began to be a major voice in the world of Theatre. Contrary to what one might assume, the first "Capital" of American Theatre was actually the City of Philadelphia, especially the works produced at Thomas Wignell's Chestnut Street Theatre. Touring theatre took root in the early 1800's along the Ohio River as Producer/Entrepreneur Samuel Drake brought plays to cities like Louisville and Lexington, Kentucky. As the Century advanced New York City ascended to dominance, migrating slowly up Broadway from the Bowery to the present location of the iconic "Broadway Theatre District" near Times Square.

In Russia "Realism" was becoming the byword in Theatre. The establishment of a distinct "Russian School" of writing and acting centered around the new conservatories and theatres set up by Prince Alexander Shakhovskoy. Inspired by the writers and actors he observed while in Paris, Shakhovskoy went on to create actual regulations which defined how theatrical troupes and centers of training should work. Ivan Turgenev and Aleksandr Ostrovsky (who has the distinction of being considered the first "professional" playwright in Russian history) strived to create drama that depicted realism onstage based upon the rise of psychology as a field of academic study. Turgenev famously said that in his work he hoped to use "domestic detail to reveal [humanity's] inner turmoil." This commitment to Realism, especially with regard to the inner psychological suffering experienced by all human beings, was the launching point for the creation of the Moscow Art Theatre, which gave the world, especially the American Theatre World, the artist whose ideas were to reconfigure the landscape of the performing arts: Konstantin Stanislavski. This man's treatises on Acting, Directing, and Play Writing took The United States by storm in the 20th Century. Stanislavski is the man who championed, along with his many contemporary Russian theatre artists, the concept that is known as "Theatrical Truth."

Finally, there are two things that must be spoken of when looking at the influence that the 19th Century had on the continuum of Theatre History. The first is a concept and the second is a man. The concept is "The Well Made Play" and the man is Norwegian Playwright Henrik Ibsen.

Simply stated the "Well Made Play" refers to a text that adheres to the theatrical rules laid out by Aristotle in his "Poetics." The idea, to review, is that a play has an arc; a distinctive beginning, middle, and end during which the audience is given Expository Information early on in the story to establish the "who what when where and why" of the play. This is followed by an Inciting Incident, which leads to an Introduction of Conflict, which leads to a Climax/Catharsis and then is tied up by the process of Denouement. The term "Well Made Play" was to many theatre professionals and artists in the 19th Century used as a derogatory term, since its adherence to a definable format didn't necessarily gibe with the concept of Realism or Theatrical Truth.

Ibsen embodied not only "Realism" but a sibling concept known as "Naturalism." Charles Darwin had published his monumental and tremendously controversial book "The Origin Of Species" in which concepts such as Evolution and Survival of the Fittest were put forth as theories which he based upon his years of world travel and empirical scientific research. This inspired Emile Zola, the French philosopher, to write a widely read essay inspired by this controversy, a controversy that found Zola firmly on Darwin's side, entitled "Naturalism in the Theatre." Zola posited that aesthetic and poetic beauty could be found all through the entire world up to and including the humble apartment of a lower class working man. Ibsen, combining the concepts of Naturalism, Realism, and using the tenets of the Aristotlean "Well Made Play", created powerful dramas with sharp social commentary including protofeminism in the iconic "A Doll's House." This drama tells the story of the dissolution of the marriage of an upper middle class couple, Torvald and Nora Helmer. It was scandalous in its day because Nora, the seemingly meek but internally intelligent, powerful, and frustrated wife of the domineering Torvald, ultimately deserts him, slamming the door as she leaves in a symbolic sonic act of castration.

On that note…Let's leap into the 20th Century and the Theatre created in this dynamic ten decades. Film of course began to be a major factor, and it would ultimately shape a great deal of how theatre was made. This was true especially after the ascendance of Talkies and innovations in recording and cinematography. Film had a great influence in the area of Acting. Screen Acting is smaller, subtler, and less overt than Stage Acting; and this created a new hybrid kind of Actor who would hopefully be able to thrive in these disparate mediums of the same essential art. Sticking strictly to what evolved upon the stage during the 20th Century it can be said that the influence of Stanislavski, and the Moscow Art Theatre's devotion to the concept of "Theatrical Truth" made tremendous waves in American stagecraft. The triumphant Moscow Art Theatre tour of Europe and the United States in 1922 exposed Western European and American audiences to the new Russian style; especially its approach to acting. The books Stanislavski wrote on the subject of Theatrical Truth and realistic acting: *My Life in Art*," "*The Actor and His Work*," "*An Actor Prepares*," "*Building a Character*," and *"Creating a Role"* are still widely read and studied, and indeed it would be hard to find a modern American Actor today who has not at least skimmed through "An Actor Prepares." Several of the budding Playwrights, Directors, Actors, and Teachers who were working and creating in New York City were dramatically influenced by this latest line of approach, and in 1932 many of these new acolytes of Realism and Theatrical Truth founded the Group Theatre. The Group Theatre was one of the great artistic game changers in Theatre and the continuum that is its History. Directors such as Elia Kazan; Actors such as John Garfield, teachers and acting theorists such as Lee Strasberg, Sanford Meisner, and Stella Adler, and playwrights such as Clifford Odets all worked within the Group Theatre and their productions. Collectively the Group Theatre is credited with developing the Method; a set of Acting techniques and dictums aimed at creating characters that were as true and believable as humanly possible. Strasberg and Meisner remain major influences in modern Acting training, even though they had fundamental disagreements between each other regarding the approach Actors should take in their work. Although they disagreed about the nuts and bolts of accomplishing it, both Strasberg and Meisner felt it to be crucial that Actors create characters onstage that are in touch with genuine feelings within the demands of Theatrical Truth. After the breakup of the Group Theatre, Meisner continued to promote his concept of Full Immersion to Actors. Meanwhile Strasberg taught classic techniques of Method Acting, many of which were based on the concept of Sense Memory (otherwise known as Gestalt.) By the 1950's Strasberg formed the Actor's Studio, which remains in operation to the present day, promoting and training professional Actors in Method technique. The list of famous Actors who have attended the Actor's Studio includes luminaries such as Paul Newman, Marilyn Monroe, James Dean, and Marlon Brando. The Meisner Technique is the backbone of many Actors training in contemporary times as well, especially those Actors who specialize primarily in Film work.

# The Pendulum; How Theatre and History Shift Through the Ages

The pendulum, or one way to look at theatre history from a stylistic point of view, is a brief thesis we asked Professor Donn Youngstrom to write. Here is what he had to say:

Theatre is as with any art form a reaction to or reflection of its particular society. If one were to take a larger view of Theatre History, there would seem to be a pendulum effect between a rational/scientific approach to theatre versus an emotional/instinctual approach. This can be seen in both plays and performance as the pendulum sways back and forth throughout the course of history. In ancient Greece you have the epic sway of Aeschylus compared to the more emotional power of Euripides with Sophocles somewhere in between. It is Sophocles and in particular his play *Oedipus Rex*, which becomes the model for Aristotle's *The Poetics*. With the "rediscovery" of Aristotle during the Renaissance both *The Poetics* along with the Roman author Horace's *The Art of Poetry* become the basis for neoclassicism. On the other hand, Euripides is much more of an influence on the Roman playwright Seneca. Seneca in turn becomes the model for Elizabethan playwrights and in particular Shakespeare who reject neoclassicism. During the medieval period plays for the most part were religious in nature—exploring the mystical elements of faith—trusting instinct over the five senses. This will later resonate during the nineteenth century with the rejection of the eighteenth century Enlightenment (and neoclassicism) and the embrace through a romantic lens of the medieval period. Romanticism emphasizes the emotional/instinctive qualities of drama—which explains the popularity of Shakespeare during this period. The opposite is true with Enlightenment philosophers like Diderot who would insist that acting should be approached in a scientific manner. Both Naturalism and Realism react to romanticism by presenting a more "realistic" world. Stanislavsky's "system" of acting is closer to Diderot's approach based on observation. By the end of the century and the beginning of the next you have the emergence of "realism" as the dominant form, while already the response to that is the anti-realism genres like symbolism, expressionism and later existentialism and absurdist theatre.

e arlier in this text, the relationship between the audience and the actors onstage was described as a contract—an agreement between the players and those who observe in which the actors promise to bring their commitment and preparation to the theatre and the audience tacitly agrees to suspend their disbelief. Ideally, this simply happens without being thought about by either party. However, in recent times, especially in the United States, a few new barriers have appeared that sometimes derail the actor/audience communication. The most challenging (and exasperating) barrier has been the cell phone. A lot of students reading this text might have just shuddered at the last sentence, anticipating a lecture from an old person about the plague of technology and how in the old days things and people were simply better. Let's be clear here: This is not going to be a diatribe about the evils of modern telecommunication. The fact is that every contributor to this book is a cell phone owner and operator. It is the communication mode of the times. Even the actors onstage have cell phones back in the dressing room. Hopefully, those phones are not with them onstage. If the actors *have* brought their cell phones into the acting area, then one hopes they are on silent. We all are living through an era of

# 21: your role as the audience

explosive and exciting new media. There is no way the genie is going back into the bottle, and society is adapting. Therefore, since theatre is a product of society, the artists who create and the audiences who witness theatre need to adapt as well.

So, to move forward with this section it is important to address the readers/ students who are seeing these words directly. For the most part the students in a typical Intro to Theatre class are between the ages of 17 and 21. Sure, there are indeed some students who are significantly older, and there may even be a rare student who is younger than 17 in a typical Intro to Theatre class. But the preponderance of people in the desks will be recent high school grads. Welcome to school, kids!

Here's the deal. Cell phones can ruin a live performance. Period. Using them during the show within the theatre is rude and inexcusable. Period. This is not just true of the theatre. It is also true of music, poetry, comedy, movies, and really any form of entertainment where people gather as a group to watch and listen. But the sad fact is that in the theatre cell phone use is at its most destructive. The ring tone, the text message tone, the sound effects of a smart phone video game, all of these are distracting, not only to the actors but to fellow audience members as well. On top of the sonic nightmare of all those aforementioned features found in phones, there is the even more catastrophic effect brought into the space by the illumination of the telephone screen. In a darkened theatre, the light thrown by a phone can make it easy for people several aisles over to read small type. The glow of the phone ruins the effects that the lighting designer (actually all of the designers, but most directly the lighting) has spent weeks or even months preparing and executing. Your phone takes focus off of the stage because it is literally a beacon in an unlit space, and that beacon points the eyes of all human beings around directly toward you. The audience member behind you has to fight over a million years of evolutionary development to take her or his eyes away from the new and unexpected stimulus of the photons and sound waves your telephone has spilled out into the room. You are being annoying and immature to the people around you, some of whom are likely to be your friends. Someone right next to you may in fact be "that someone" who piques your romantic interest. They aren't impressed by your dismal behavior.

And what it does to the actors? Well, what it does to the actors is perhaps the single most pernicious thing about using a cell phone in a theatre.

From the stage, the glow of a cell phone in the audience is a retina-burning distraction and a disheartening confidence drain in the actor's mind. Seeing that blue green glow out in the darkness of the theatre is a direct message to the performers which says, "You are not engaging me and I am not watching." It is, simply stated, incredibly rude and disrespectful. It is just plain mean. Rather than sitting in the seats talking or texting, most actors would prefer you would just walk up onstage and slap them. It wouldn't hurt their egos anywhere near as much if you did that. It would at least give the actors a chance to redress your insulting behavior in a direct manner. Once again, using the metaphor of a contract, the cell phone users in the audience are in breach. Suspension of disbelief cannot occur in a distracted mind because ultimately, being undistracted *is what suspension of disbelief actually is*. To bring in the other half of the contract, the preparation, training, concentration, and commitment of the actors onstage, it is not exaggeration to say that being distracted by impolite audience members can eviscerate a show. For actors onstage who are trying to bring their fullest concentration to the performance, distraction is an absolute deal breaker.

Again, let's go back to the terms of the deal between those who watch and those who present.

If you ask an actor what the single most common question they are asked after any performance is, they will tell you it is this: "How do you remember all of those lines?" It is a question that can exasperate a performer, but it is not in any way a dumb question. Remembering a part is, indeed, quite a daunting chore. According to most sources, the play *Hamlet* has almost 30 thousand words, and anywhere from 35 to 40 percent of those words are spoken by the character Hamlet himself. That means that in order to memorize the role of Hamlet, an actor has to learn at least 10,500 words! Indeed, "How do you remember?" is not necessarily a dumb query. The reason that particular question annoys actors sometimes is because learning the lines is the *least* an actor does. After dozens of rehearsals and after putting in the required work, it is hard *not* to know the lines, truth be told. The job of playing a part includes—but is so much more than—memorization of words. Those words must be interpreted. They have to be analyzed and their meaning defined. The actor has to make choices that are informed by those words. Those words have to be clearly enunciated. They have to be a part of a fully realized character who is active and reacts to the words and actions of other characters in the play.

An actor with the good fortune (the privilege, really) of getting to play an iconic role like Hamlet is going to put perhaps hundreds of hours into preparation for opening night. This includes research, rehearsal, fight choreography, physical fitness (this is a role that takes an enormous physical toll on the actor—hit the gym!), and yes, memorization. All of that hard work is culminated on opening night and continues until the production closes. The actor playing the role cannot skimp on the work and his portrayal of Hamlet has to be real, effective, and believable. And that individual character of Hamlet is just one part of the tale to be told. The entire story of the play has to be sharp and accessible to the outside world. All of the characters, not just Hamlet, must bring all of their skill and effort into the fray, along with their complete commitment and concentration. All of this is expected to occur, night after night, in real time in front of a live audience. There is so much an actor is asked to give in order to create a believable role. Without all of the elements, it is impossible for the play to thrive and entertain and inform. And then, after all of this work and sacrifice, somebody in the house wants to sit and talk on a phone? And on top of that, the texters and call takers expect the show to go on despite their intrusive clumsiness? Talk about unlikely …

A good performance is absolutely out of the question if the artists cannot concentrate. All of the work, all of the commitment—heck, all of the fun—goes away when an audience member interrupts a play with a call or a text. So as audience members, if you do not turn your phone off, you are actually cheating yourself. You are excluding yourself from the best version of the experience. Why do that? Why pay for a ticket and ruin the fun? Nobody would ask a heart surgeon to do her or his best work while being annoyed, so why would consumers of art expect it to be acceptable to interrupt the artists? Look at your ticket. See that number with a dollar sign next to it? That's right. You've paid for the expertise of the actors! You've entrusted them with your evening's entertainment. Therefore, if you are rude and disruptive, well, quite literally, you are wasting your own time and money. As a coda to all of this, it is important to also mention something we all learned in kindergarten. Being rude simply is not nice. A grown-up doesn't treat other people with disrespect. Do unto others in the audience as you would have them do unto you.

Besides the value of the artistic experience and the performer/audience contract, there is another real, tangible benefit to turning off your phone at a play. The Internet, as well as cellular phone technology and the cloud, are all good things that can greatly enhance our lives. Again, the author of this chapter and all of the authors of this book are members of the same society as you. We own and use phones, computers, and tablets; we will most likely be consumers of whatever technologies ultimately replace them. Communication technology has immense potential for good. However, the potential for misuse is also real, and it goes further than just being rude to actors and other theatregoers. Being perpetually in contact means that we are no longer allowed solitude. We aren't allowed to be out of touch, to have time and experiences that are entirely our own. Somebody can always reach us—even if we are lying on a boulder in the Theodore Roosevelt National Park, watching wild bison tread by on a hot September day.[1]

It is not unlikely that every reader of this book experiences the occasional need to be *out of touch* with the outside world. In fact, it is beyond the limits of imagination that there are people who do not crave solitude. It is hard to believe there could be a person who doesn't desire time to think. (Or even better, *not to think*.) All people desire, from time to time, to be unreachable. Toward that end, theatre presents a perfect opportunity when you think about it. Sitting in a comfortable seat watching good actors perform a well-written play with solid direction, witnessing a live spectacle with high production values and perhaps music or maybe even special effects, is sublime. The sanctuary of the theatre offers every human being in the space a time-out from life and its inherent stress. We can declare our right to solitude; we can exercise our right to enjoy an experience that is enlightening, entertaining, and most of all, *UNINTERRUPTED*. The announcement at the beginning of the production ("Please turn off all cell phones and electronic devices.") is our excuse to slip away from our lives for a little while and let our imaginative childlike minds have the reins. It's okay! We can let ourselves go, let ourselves enter a different world, the world of the play. Our credit scores and commitments can take a hike for a few hours. We can veg out. We can subconsciously quote Curt Cobain and send his message psychically toward the stage: "Here we are now. Entertain us."

Anyone who is mad at us for not immediately responding to a call or a text can be told that we were asked to turn the phone off. We can reassure those who wanted our attention that missing that call or text was nothing personal. If we, the audience, are willing to claim it, the theatre offers us a glorious opportunity to step out of our lives for a few hours. This is not something unimportant or esoteric, and it is in no way meant to be ironic. Solitude is necessary to our being. It is an essential part of the human experience. Going back once again to the contract metaphor, it is the ultimate value of the actor/audience transaction: If we give ourselves over without distraction to the play, then we, the audience, get to experience the theatrical art to its fullest. We get the complete reward of the creative work of the acting company. The theatre and the production owes us that. It is implied by the price of the ticket. And what do we have to do to get it? What is our end of the agreement? Simple. We just have to watch and listen—without distraction.

In short, turn that cell phone off and enjoy the show! It is what you paid for, and it is what the artists are paid to do for you. After the curtain call, you can turn the little monster back on and check back into the electronic universe. TTYL …

---

1   The author, in real life, had this experience. In the quiet of a perfect Great Plains Badlands afternoon, surrounded by glorious wildlife, the idyllic moment was interrupted by the ringing of the telephone in his pocket.

## Abstraction

The quality of dealing with ideas rather than events.

## Aesthetics

An artistically beautiful or pleasing appearance.

## Algonguin Round Table

The Algonquin Round Table was a celebrated group of New York City writers, critics, actors and wits.

## Antebellum Era

Occurring in the Southern U.S. during the time before the American Civil War.

# glossary

## Backing

Support or aid: financial backing.

## Bullpen

In Baseball, an area where relief pitchers warm up during a game.

## Cubism

A movement in 20th-century painting in which several planes of an object in the form of cubes or other solids are presented in an arbitrary arrangement using a narrow range of colors or monochrome.

## Dadaism

A European artistic and literary movement (1916–1923) that flouted conventional aesthetic and cultural values by producing works marked by nonsense, travesty, and incongruity.

## Dark Night

A night the theatre is not being used for a show.

## Equity

The Actors' Equity Association (AEA), commonly referred to as Actors' Equity or simply Equity, is an American labor union representing the world of live theatrical performance.

## Martin Esslin

(6 June 1918–24 February 2002) was a Hungarian-born English producer and playright dramatist, journalist, adaptor and translator, critic, academic scholar and professor of drama best known for coining the term "Theatre of the Absurd" in his work of that name.

## Festival of Dionysus

The Dionysia was a large festival in ancient Athens in honor of the god Dionysus, the central event of which was the performance of tragedies and, from 487 BC, comedies. It was the second-most important festival after the Panathenaia. The Dionysia actually comprised two related festivals, the Rural Dionysia and the City Dionysia, which took place in different parts of the year. They were also an essential part of the Dionysian Mysteries.

## Fiduciary

An individual in whom another has placed the utmost trust and confidence to manage and protect property or money. The relationship wherein one person has an obligation to act for another's benefit.

## Fin de Siecle Salons of Paris:

The term "fin de siècle" is commonly applied to French art and artists as the traits of the culture first appeared there, but the movement affected many European countries at the end of the 19th Century.

## Hedda Gabler

A play first published in 1890 by Norwegian playwright Henrik Ibsen.

## House Lights

The lights that illuminate the audience section of a concert hall, theater, or auditorium.

## Intuitive

The act or faculty of knowing or sensing without the use of rational processes; immediate cognition.

## Kinetic Energy

Form is not only composed of energy, it also uses that energy to move itself. In this process form becomes theatrical, for what is theatre but the "imitation of an action" as Aristotle pointed out many centuries before modern physics. Energy then both comprises form and provides the impetus for that form to move.

## Lort Theatre

League of Resident Theatres.

## Ohm's Law

The law was named after the German physicist Georg Ohm, who, in a treatise published in 1827, described measurements of applied voltage and current through simple electrical circuits containing various lengths of wire.

## OSHA

A federal Agency that oversees Occupational Safety and Health.

## Photometrics

The science of the measurement of light, in terms of its perceived brightness to the human eye.

## Pop Art

A form of art that depicts objects or scenes from everyday life and employs techniques of commercial art and popular illustration.

## Rendering

to reproduce or represent by artistic or verbal means.

## Surrealism

20th-century literary and artistic movement that attempts to express the workings of the subconscious and is characterized by fantastic imagery and incongruous juxtaposition of subject matter.

## Temporal

Relating to the sequence of time or to a particular time.

# Image credits

## Images in order of appearance:

0  1341  1571803  0

CPSIA information can be obtained at www.ICGtesting.com
Printed in the USA
LVOW02s2148120914

403911LV00001B/1/P

9  781626  617841